AN INTRODUCTION TO

Sports Physiology

A home study pack providing sportspeople with
an introduction to how the body works during exercise

Copyright © sports coach UK, 2003

First published 1995 by the National Coaching Foundation
Revised 1996 and 1999 by the National Coaching Foundation

This document is copyright under the Berne Convention. All rights are reserved. Apart from any fair dealing for the purpose of private study, research, criticism or review, as permitted under the Copyright, Designs and Patents Act, 1988, no part of this publication may be reproduced, stored in a retrieval system, or transmitted in any form or by any means, electronic, electrical, chemical, mechanical, optical, photocopying, recording or otherwise, without the prior written permission of the copyright owner. Enquiries should be addressed to **Coachwise Solutions**.

ISBN 1-902523-65-2

Author: Martin Farrally
Editor: Penny Crisfield
Typesetter: Sandra Flintham
Illustrations: William Rudling
Cover photo courtesy of actionplus sports images

sports coach UK
114 Cardigan Road
Headingley
Leeds LS6 3BJ
Tel: 0113-274 4802 Fax: 0113-275 5019
E-mail: coaching@sportscoachuk.org
Website: www.sportscoachuk.org

Patron: HRH The Princess Royal

In conjunction with

sportscotland
Caledonia House
South Gyle
Edinburgh EH12 9DQ

Published on behalf of
sports coach UK by

Coachwise Solutions
Coachwise Ltd
Chelsea Close
Off Amberley Road
Armley
Leeds LS12 4HP
Tel: 0113-231 1310 Fax: 0113-231 9606
E-mail: enquiries@coachwisesolutions.co.uk
Website: www.coachwisesolutions.co.uk

Preface

This home study pack, produced by the National Coaching Foundation in conjunction with **sport**scotland, complements two other packs in the series: *An Introduction to the Structure of the Body* (functional anatomy) and *An Introduction to Sports Mechanics*.

It is intended for anyone (coach, teacher, performer) who wishes to understand how the body functions during exercise. This is essential in designing fitness programmes, and planning coaching and training sessions. Each chapter provides information, activities and questions to help you. If this information is new to you, the pack will probably take between 15–20 hours to complete.

By completing the pack, you will be able to generate some evidence towards the underpinning knowledge and application required for Level 3 National Occupational Standards for Coaching, Teaching and Instructing (see Appendix D for further details).

Key to symbols used in the text:

 An activity.

 Approximate length of time to be spent on the activity.

 Stop and consider.

 Self tester questions to check your own understanding.

Throughout this pack, the pronouns he, she, him, her and so on are interchangeable and intended to be inclusive of both men and women. It is important in sport, as elsewhere, that men and women have equal opportunities.

Contents

		Page
Chapter One	**Introduction**	1
1.0	What's in It for You?	1
1.1	Getting Started	2
1.2	Overview of the Pack	5
1.3	Recap	6
1.4	What Next?	6
Chapter Two	**Overview of the Oxygen Transport System**	7
2.0	What's in It for You?	7
2.1	Why is an Oxygen Transport System Needed?	10
2.2	Loading the Oxygen Transport System with Oxygen	12
2.3	Moving Blood to Where it is Needed	18
2.4	Returning Blood to the Heart	22
2.5	Recap	24
2.6	What Next?	28
Chapter Three	**Coping with Exercise**	29
3.0	What's in It for You?	29
3.1	Lungs	29
3.2	Blood	35
3.3	Heart	46
3.4	Muscle Use of Oxygen	52
3.5	Recap	54
3.6	What Next?	57
Chapter Four	**Training Oxygen Transport and Utilisation**	59
4.0	What's in It for You?	59
4.1	Principles of Training	60
4.2	Key Principles for Aerobic Training	64
4.3	Adaptations with Aerobic Training	82
4.4	Recap	85
4.5	What Next?	90

		Page
Chapter Five	Energy	91
	5.0 What's in It for You?	91
	5.1 Adenosine Triphosphate (ATP)	92
	5.2 Anaerobic Energy Systems	94
	5.3 Aerobic Energy Systems	102
	5.4 Contribution of each Energy System	105
	5.5 Application to your Sport	108
	5.6 Recap	113
	5.7 What Next?	117
Appendix A	Multiple Choice Questions	121
Appendix B	Case Study	125
Appendix C	National Occupational Standards for Coaching, Teaching and Instructing	127

CHAPTER ONE
Introduction

1.0 What's in It for You?

Physiology is the study of how the body functions. In the home study pack *An Introduction to the Structure of the Body*[1], the way muscles are structured and how force is developed through contraction were explained. This home study pack will describe how oxygen is supplied from the air and used by the working muscles, and how the energy from food is used as muscle fuel. When you have completed the pack, you should have a better understanding of the physiological demands of your sport and be more able to prepare relevant fitness training programmes. In particular, you should be able to:

- explain the importance of oxygen, how it is transported from the atmosphere to the working muscles and used by the muscles to do work
- describe how the oxygen transport system responds to exercise and adapts with training
- describe how energy is made available to fuel movement, identify the energy sources most relevant to your sport, and know how to ensure that the body stores of energy are maximised prior to competition
- design an aerobic training programme suitable for a performer in your sport.

This chapter will provide an overview of the content of the pack and prepare you for the later chapters. By the end of this chapter, you should be able to:

- state the purpose of the pack and its contents
- assess whether or not you need to do some background reading as preparation
- start a glossary of terms to which you can add as you work through the pack to help with new terminology.

---

1 Available from Coachwise Ltd (0113 231 1310).

―――――――― CHAPTER ONE ――――――――

1.1 Getting Started

In preparation for this pack, you should be familiar with the contents of the NCF Introductory Study Pack *The Body in Action* and have some understanding of the structure of the heart, lungs and blood-vessels. You may also find it helpful to have completed the home study pack *An Introduction to the Structure of the Body*. Activity 1 will help you assess if you have this essential knowledge and how to gain further information if necessary.

ACTIVITY 1

1   Fill in the missing words:

   To obtain circulation, there needs to be a pump to push the _____ around the body. This is the function of the _____. A system of _____ distributes the blood to where it is needed, and the mechanism to ensure the blood flows in only one direction is provided by the _____. The human body really has two circulating systems; the pulmonary circulation delivering blood to the _____ to pick up _____ and off-load carbon dioxide and water, and the systemic circulation to the rest of the _____.

2   One function of the circulatory system is to transport food and oxygen to working muscles and organs. List at least two other functions:

   •

   •

   •

   •

CHAPTER ONE

3   The oxygen which passes from the atmosphere down into the lungs is conducted along a series of tubes before entering the bloodstream. Rewrite the following list of structures to show how the air is conducted into the blood:

- Air
- Trachea
- Alveolus
- Larynx
- Bronchiole
- Mouth/nose
- Bronchi
- Air sac
- Bloodstream

- Air
-
-
-
-
-
-
-
- Bloodstream

4   The heart is made up of four chambers. Draw a simple diagram of the heart showing these four chambers and the blood-vessels linked to them. Give the names of the chambers and blood-vessels:

Now turn over.

CHAPTER ONE

Compare your answers with the following:

1 *To obtain circulation there needs to be a pump to push the **blood** around the body. This is the function of the **heart**. A system of **blood-vessels** distributes the blood to where it is needed, and the mechanism to ensure the blood flows in only one direction is provided by the **valves**. The human body really has two circulating systems: the pulmonary circulation delivering blood to the **lungs** to pick up **oxygen** and off-load carbon dioxide and water, and the systemic circulation to the rest of the **body**.*

2 *The other functions of the circulatory system are:*
   - *maintaining the fluid balance of the body*
   - *removing waste products*
   - *transporting heat to maintain body temperature*
   - *transporting hormones.*

3
   - *Air*
   - *Mouth/nose*
   - *Larynx*
   - *Trachea*
   - *Bronchi*
   - *Bronchiole*
   - *Air sac*
   - *Alveolus*
   - *Bloodstream.*

4

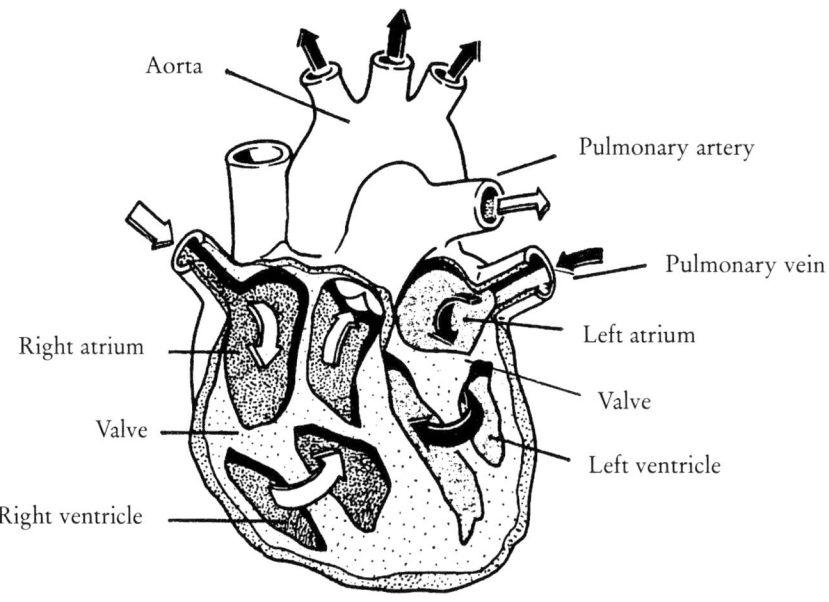

Figure 1: The heart

The questions concentrated on the structure of the oxygen transport system. If you found them difficult, or feel you would like to know more about the basic anatomy of the heart, lungs and blood-vessels, consult a general anatomy and physiology textbook aimed at senior pupils or first year students (see Section 1.4). You may find it helpful to have such a textbook to hand as you work through this pack.

Although this pack has been written with a minimum of jargon and technical language, you are likely to meet quite a number of terms which are new to you. The following activity has been designed as a *jargon buster*.

ACTIVITY 2

You will find it helpful, and a boost to your confidence, if you build your own glossary as you work through the text. You should write your glossary on a separate sheet of paper so that you can keep it with you as you work through the pack. Try to use your own words so that the term is explained in a way you can understand and remember.

Here are some words to start you off.

Their term	**My definition**
Bronchi/bronchiole	A tube in the lungs.
System	A large part of the body, such as the heart and blood-vessels (circulatory system), which carries out a special task.
Trachea	Windpipe.

1.2   Overview of the Pack

The remainder of the pack has been divided into four separate chapters. By working through them, you will be able to develop your knowledge about the physiology of the body so that you can design a training programme to meet the physiological demands of your sport.

Oxygen Transport System

All human cells need oxygen to stay alive and use energy. In **Chapter Two**, you will find out about the structures in the body which transport the oxygen from the air to the muscles so that they can work.

Transporting and Using Oxygen

Exercise places the body under stress. In **Chapter Three**, you will discover how the oxygen transport system speeds up the delivery of oxygen to meet the needs of the exercising body.

Training Oxygen Transport and Utilisation

The purpose of training is to make the work easier to do, and to be able to achieve more when working as hard as possible. **Chapter Four** will explain the principles of training, how to design your training programmes, and what changes to expect in the body.

Energy

Oxygen is not the fuel for movement, only the means by which energy can be released from the stores in the muscle. **Chapter Five** will enable you to explain how energy is made available in a variety of different sporting situations, and how to design training programmes for your sport to maximise the storage and use of energy.

1.3 Recap

From this introductory chapter, you should now be clear about the contents of the remainder of this pack and have started a glossary to come to terms with the inevitable jargon in sports physiology. You have been able to check your own knowledge and understanding of the body and if you have any doubts about your readiness to continue with this pack, you are encouraged to work through the recommended packs in the next section.

1.4 What Next?

You may find it helpful to review the contents of the following packs:

Bursztyn, PG and Jack, PG (1990) **Physiology for sportspeople: a serious user's guide to the body.** Manchester, Manchester University Press. ISBN 0-7190-3086-2. *(Out of print)*

Farrally, M (1995) **An introduction to the structure of the body.** Leeds, National Coaching Foundation. ISBN 1-85060-1690. *

McArdle, WD, Katch, FI and Katch, VL (1996) **Exercise physiology: energy, nutrition, and human performance.** 4th edition. New York, Lippincott Williams. ISBN 0-68318-103-3.

National Coaching Foundation (1997) **Physiology and performance.** 3rd edition. Leeds, National Coaching Foundation. ISBN 0-947850-24-4. *

National Coaching Foundation (1993) **The body in action.** 3rd edition. Leeds, National Coaching Foundation. ISBN 0-947850-51-1. *

---

* Available from Coachwise Ltd (0113 231 1310).

CHAPTER TWO
Overview of the Oxygen Transport System

2.0 What's in It for You?

The human body cannot function unless there is an adequate supply of oxygen or the shortfall can be made up quickly. Consequently, if exercise is to continue for any length of time, the delivery systems have to speed up their supply of oxygen to the working tissues. If insufficient oxygen is supplied, the body will slow down or stop the activity after a short time and then have to make up the oxygen debt (repay the oxygen deficit).

Later chapters will show how the oxygen transport system responds to exercise and adapts with training, and how energy is released by the muscle. First it is important to look more closely at the system and how it works.

By the end of this chapter, you should be able to:

- describe the pathway of oxygen from the atmosphere to the muscles
- identify the structures which make up the oxygen transport system
- state the constituents of blood and what it carries
- explain how the blood is moved to the working muscles and returned to the heart.

CHAPTER TWO

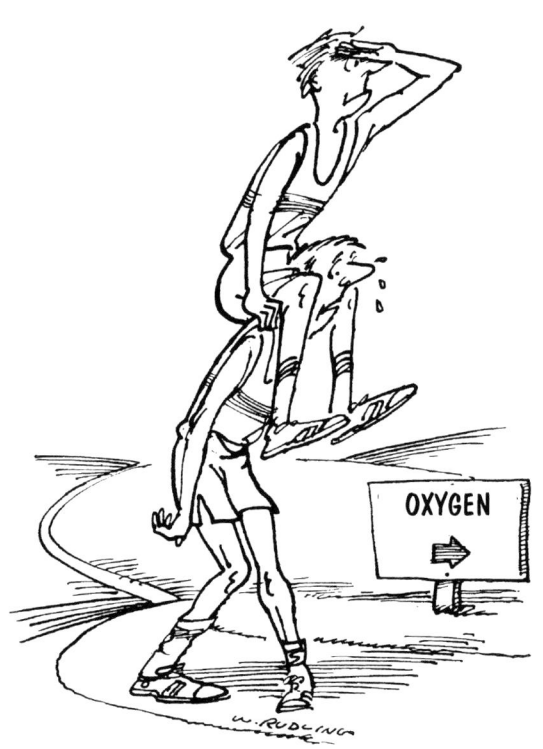

The crucial role that oxygen plays in any physical activity can be readily seen when you start to exercise. Try the next activity.

ACTIVITY 3

1. While you are sitting quietly reading this, fill in the table which asks you to focus on the following body parts and note down anything that you feel or notice. For example, are you aware of air movement in your mouth or nose? If so, note down in what way. Leave the two right-hand columns blank for the moment.

Part of Body	Aware While Sitting?	In What Way?	Aware After Exercise?	In What Way?
Mouth/nose				
Chest				
Heart/pulse				
Working muscles				

2. Now do some exercise for about five minutes (eg run up the stairs, jog, do some aerobics) and then immediately fill in the remaining two columns.

Now turn over.

You will have become much more aware of your body systems after exercising. More air is being moved in and out of the lungs, as shown by the increase in both the rate and depth of breathing. Although at rest you may have been oblivious to your beating heart or vibrating pulse, it is likely that exercise brought these to your attention. Perhaps less obvious was the change in distribution of blood. You may have detected that more was flowing to your skin because you were becoming warmer, but did you observe that your working muscles were larger because blood flow had increased? All of these changes were necessary to sustain the exercise.

2.1 Why is an Oxygen Transport System Needed?

All living cells require oxygen and energy and produce waste products. In very small, primitive living organisms (eg an amoeba), this can be provided by seepage (diffusion) through the outer walls. In a human the distance from the inner cells to the environment is too great and the demands too large for this to be effective. To overcome this problem, animals have a circulating system which communicates closely with every living cell and has the capacity to vary its delivery to meet the range of demand from rest to maximal exercise. This is the oxygen transport system shown below in Figure 2.

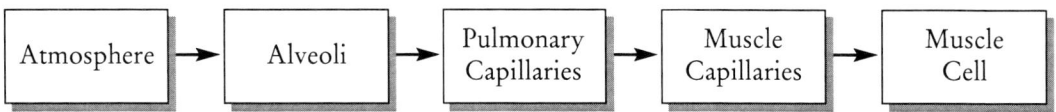

Figure 2: Oxygen transport system

As the diagram shows, the oxygen transport system comprises the lungs, heart and blood-vessels. The lungs remove carbon dioxide from the blood and load it with oxygen, the blood transports the oxygen and carbon dioxide, and it is delivered to the working tissues by the heart and blood-vessels (Figure 3 on the opposite page provides a more expanded diagram).

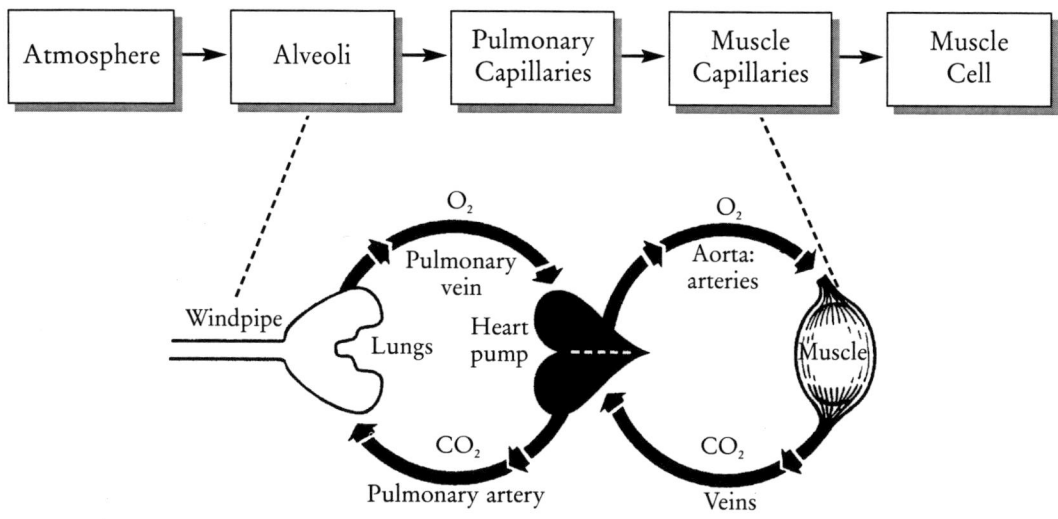

Figure 3: Oxygen transport system (expanded)

If you are unsure about the basic concepts covered so far, stop and complete the next activity.

ACTIVITY 4

Complete the table by naming the three components of the oxygen transport system and explaining what they do:

Component	Purpose
Heart	

Check your answers by rereading Section 2.1.

2.2 Loading the Oxygen Transport System with Oxygen

It is the function of the lungs to take oxygen from the atmosphere and move it into the bloodstream. This is done by conducting air down the respiratory passages as far as the air sac, allowing the oxygen to pass through the folded walls of the air sac (each fold is known as an **alveolus**) through the walls of the blood capillary, and into the red blood cells. At the same time, carbon dioxide moves from the blood into the alveolus and out into the atmosphere. Figure 4 illustrates these structures.

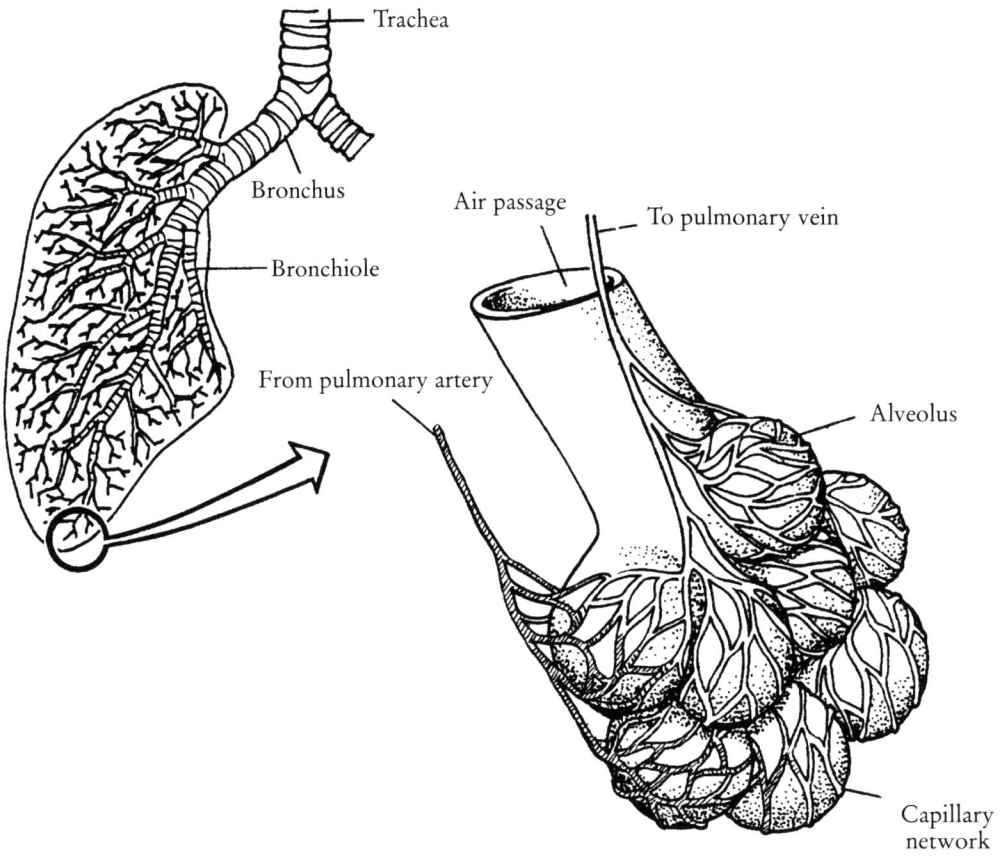

Figure 4: The lungs

How is the air moved in and out? At rest there seems to be hardly any breathing at all. Are you aware of your breathing as you read this sentence? Yet during exercise there are occasions when your lungs seem to be bursting. Try the next activity.

ACTIVITY 5

Lie on your back, relax and think about your breathing. Jot down your findings for each of the following:

1. How is air entering your lungs? Examine different parts of your body to see what is moving and what is not.

2. How much air is moving in and out of your lungs?

3. Hold your breath for as long as you can. When you breathed again was it to breathe in or out?

4. Breathe in and out rapidly and deeply about ten times in 15 seconds and then hold your breath. Could you hold your breath for much longer?
   NB Stop if you start to feel dizzy.

Now turn over.

*At rest you only need about half a litre of air every breath and you breathe about 12–20 times a minute. This **tidal volume**[1] will increase as you exercise to meet the demands for more oxygen, and will reach a maximum of about two litres in untrained women and three litres in untrained men. This is only about 50% of the maximal capacity of the lungs, which suggests that breathing may not be the limiting factor in intense exercise. You will have noticed that at rest your chest does not move but if you observed carefully, you will have seen (or felt) the front of your abdomen moving in and out in time with your breathing.*

The lungs are made from a tissue that is elastic but is unable to contract. They change in volume by responding to pressure changes between the inside and outside of the lungs and this pressure change is brought about by changing the shape of the chest (the **thoracic cavity**). It is important to remember that the chest is a sealed unit in which the lungs hang. The following diagram shows a simplified illustration of this structure.

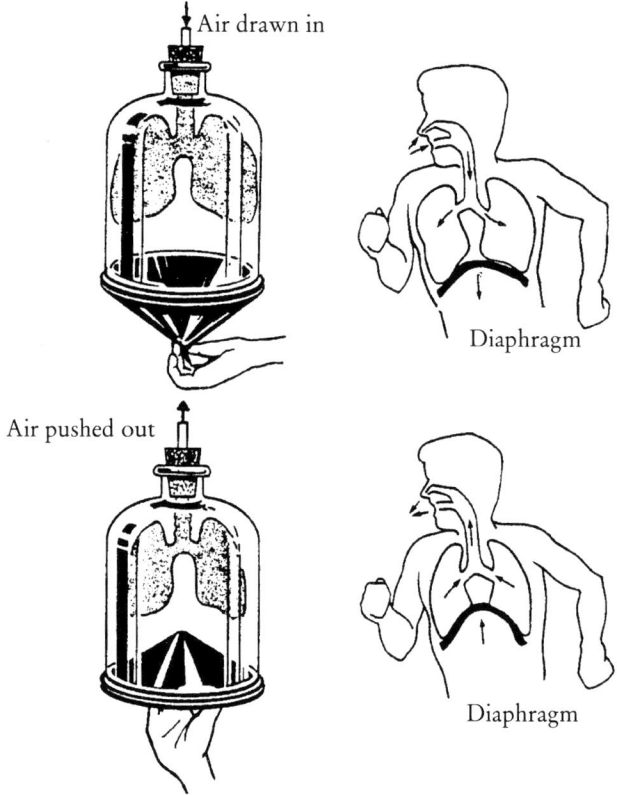

Figure 5: The thorax

As the thorax expands in response to muscles contracting, the volume in the lungs increases and the pressure drops. This draws air into the lungs. To breathe out, the muscles relax, the thorax returns to its original size and air is forced out by the increased pressure in the lungs.

---

1   Have you been keeping your glossary up to date?

You may have wondered why a punctured lung is so dangerous. If there is a hole between either the outside of the body and the thorax, or the thorax and the lung, it is impossible to create a pressure difference and so change the shape of the lung. If the lungs cannot enlarge or shrink, the air in the alveoli cannot be changed and the blood will receive no oxygen.

Why is it that only your abdomen moves at rest? It should be self-evident that you do not need to lift the rib cage to enlarge the thorax sufficiently in quiet breathing but something must move. At the base of the thoracic cavity is the diaphragm (see Figure 6). The diaphragm is a tough, tendinous dome with muscular walls which divides the thorax from the abdomen. In quiet breathing, the muscular walls of the diaphragm contract to pull the dome down and this is enough to enlarge the thorax, causing the lungs to expand sufficiently to draw in the required amount of air. As the dome of the diaphragm is pulled down into the abdomen, the pressure in the abdominal cavity increases, causing the stomach wall to move out, as you observed. In exercise you need to move greater volumes of air so muscles contract to move the rib cage.

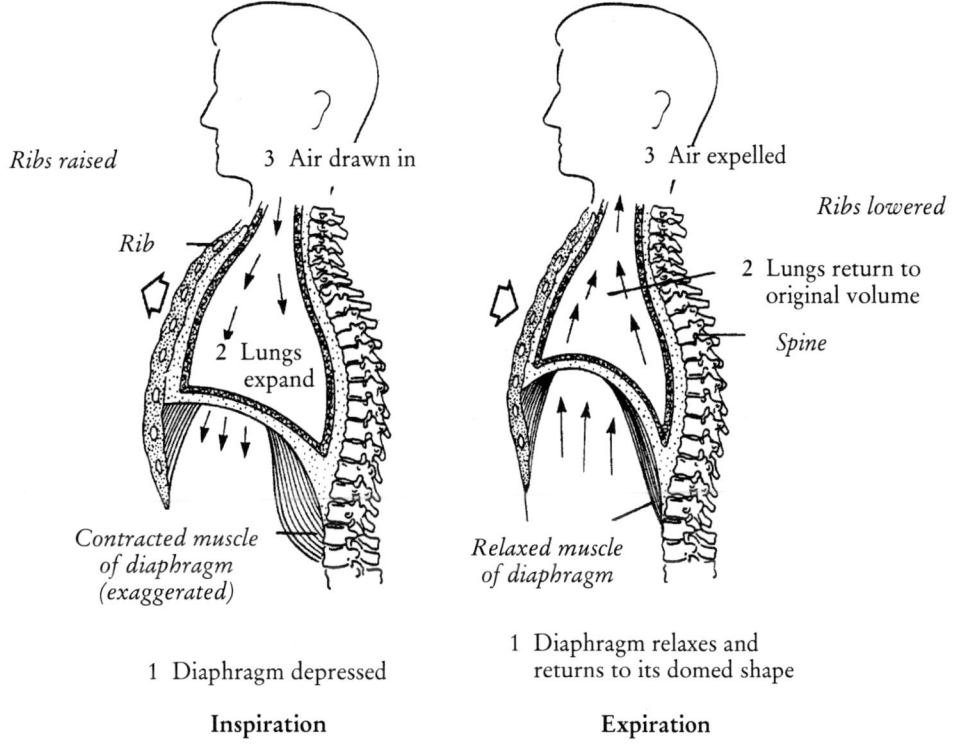

Figure 6: Quiet breathing

Think about what causes you to breathe.

When you were lying down, was it the desire to breathe in or breathe out that made you breathe again?

What happened when you held your breath?

Why is it that you were able to hold your breath for longer after you breathed in and out more rapidly than normal?

Contrary to what is often thought, your body is not very responsive to a shortage of oxygen. Breathing is controlled far more by the need to get rid of carbon dioxide rather than take in oxygen. After holding your breath, it is likely that your first desire was to breathe out so that the concentration of carbon dioxide in your blood could be reduced. The ability to hold your breath for longer after ten breaths in 15 seconds (this extra breathing is known as **hyperventilating**) is because you have driven off carbon dioxide from the blood and it takes a little while for the concentration to increase back to the normal level. The respiratory control centre in the base of the brain receives information about the level of carbon dioxide in the blood and the fluid bathing the brain. The receptors which detect these changes are very sensitive to carbon dioxide concentration, less so to changes in the amount of oxygen.

The air in the alveolus is being continually refreshed by the breathing cycle. As oxygen leaves on its way to the bloodstream, it is being replaced by oxygen arriving down the respiratory passages. Similarly, carbon dioxide is arriving constantly from the blood and being moved onwards towards the atmosphere. As a consequence, the mix of gases in the alveolus remains relatively constant and this situation can be maintained quite well in exercise because the rate and depth of breathing increases. Rapid diffusion of gases between alveolus and blood is possible because the outside of the alveolus is wrapped in a dense network of capillaries (Figure 7). It is as if a sheet of blood is washing over the alveolus.

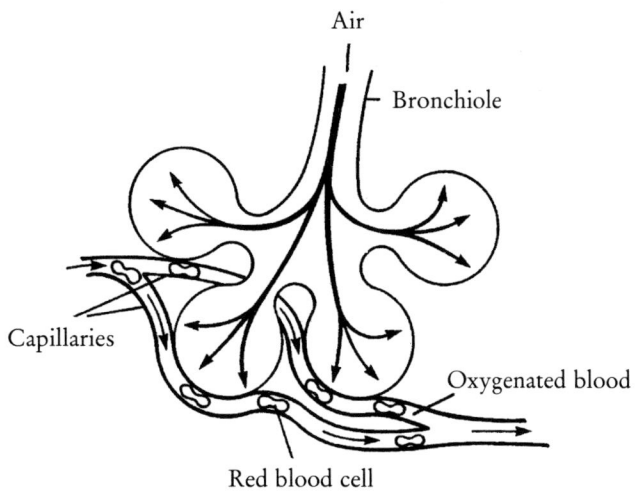

Figure 7: Capillaries passing over one alveolus

Blood is made up of:

- fluid (the **plasma**)
- cells, of which red cells are the most common.

It is the red cells which transport the oxygen because they contain **haemoglobin**, a substance with a great affinity for oxygen. The blood passes across the alveolus wall in about 0.75 seconds at rest and this gives sufficient time for it to be fully loaded with oxygen. The oxygen passes through the blood plasma and is attached to the haemoglobin which forms about one-third of the red cells. In exercise the blood is flowing much faster to speed up delivery to the working muscles but even here there is sufficient time, about 0.25 seconds in heavy exercise, for the red cells to be almost completely saturated with oxygen. Consequently, there is limited value in attempting to improve oxygen transport by breathing higher concentrations of oxygen (except of course, where the available oxygen is in short supply, as at altitude).

If you want to check your understanding, try the next activity.

ACTIVITY 6

Answer true or false to the following questions.

1. The lungs are made from a tissue which can contract to move air in and out. — True / False

2. The need to breathe comes about because of a shortage of oxygen. — True / False

3. In exercise the concentration of oxygen in the blood leaving the lungs drops considerably. — True / False

Now turn over.

You should have answered 'false' to each question. Reread Section 2.2 if you had any difficulty.

2.3 Moving Blood to Where it is Needed

Blood is no more than a transport system carrying foodstuffs, heat, hormones, water, oxygen, carbon dioxide and waste products. The pie chart below shows its constituent parts and it can be seen that most of it is water. Almost all the oxygen is transported attached to haemoglobin in the red cells, the remainder being in solution, whereas most of the carbon dioxide is carried by the water.

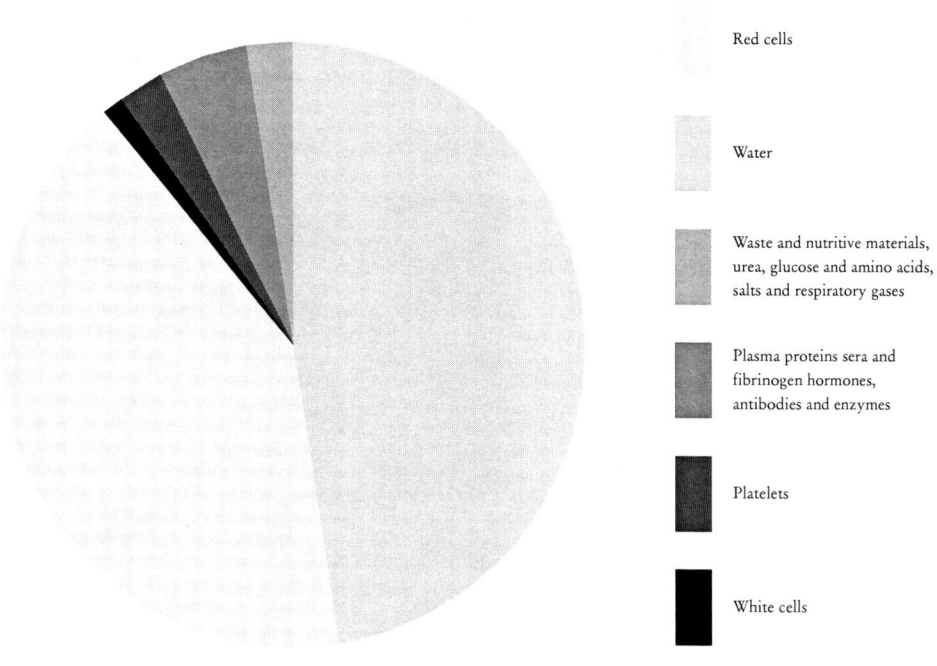

Figure 8: Constituents of blood

When the blood leaves the lungs it is almost fully saturated with oxygen even in heavy exercise. However, when the blood returns to the lungs, it is by no means devoid of all oxygen. At rest it may still be over 50% saturated with oxygen and although the percentage will drop as the intensity of exercise increases, it never falls to zero.

This is because the blood returning to the lungs is a mixture of blood from different parts of the body, and some of this blood will have passed through resting tissue, giving up very little of its oxygen.

Even if you were to examine blood leaving a large muscle working at its maximal capacity, it is likely that there would be some oxygen present because the capillary network in the muscle is not capable of ensuring that all the blood passes close to contracting muscle fibres. Also, not all fibres are capable of using large supplies of oxygen and therefore do not exhaust the blood[1]. One of the outcomes of endurance training is that muscle improves its ability to extract and use oxygen, as will be shown later.

The delivery of blood to the working tissue and return to the lungs can only be achieved if there is a circulating system. In fact, there are two which meet at the heart. Try the next activity.

ACTIVITY 7

Write in the name of the equivalent structure in the human body, which make up the circulation system:

Mechanical System	In the Body
Pump	
Tubes	
Valves	
Fluid	

Now turn over.

---

1 You may wish to refer back to the section on fibre types in *An Introduction to the Structure of the Body*.

CHAPTER TWO

Check your answers with the following table:

Mechanical System	In the Body
Pump	*Heart*
Tubes	*Blood-vessels*
Valves	*Valves*
Fluid	*Blood*

The heart is not one pump but two. The left side is by far the larger and stronger, and pumps the blood around the body systems (hence it is called the **systemic circulation**). The right side is a smaller pump pushing the blood around the lungs (the **pulmonary circulation**). The blood-vessels act as the tubes, the arteries conducting the blood away from the heart to the capillary bed, and the veins returning blood to the heart. The valves are essential for uni-directional flow and are found in the heart and veins but not in the arteries. Blood is the fluid.

Figure 9 on the opposite page shows the structure of the heart. The atria are collecting sacs to store blood waiting to enter the ventricles when they are in contraction and the valve between atria and ventricles is shut. When the ventricle contracts at rest, it will expel only a proportion of the blood contained in it. The blood is forced out of the heart into either the aorta or the pulmonary artery which has to stretch to accommodate it, forming what might be described as a temporary third chamber. The pressure of the blood at this time is at its highest (**systolic pressure**) and gradually declines as the walls of the aorta and pulmonary artery recoil and the blood moves on down the system. Just prior to the next contraction of the heart (systole), the pressure reaches its lowest point (**diastolic pressure**).

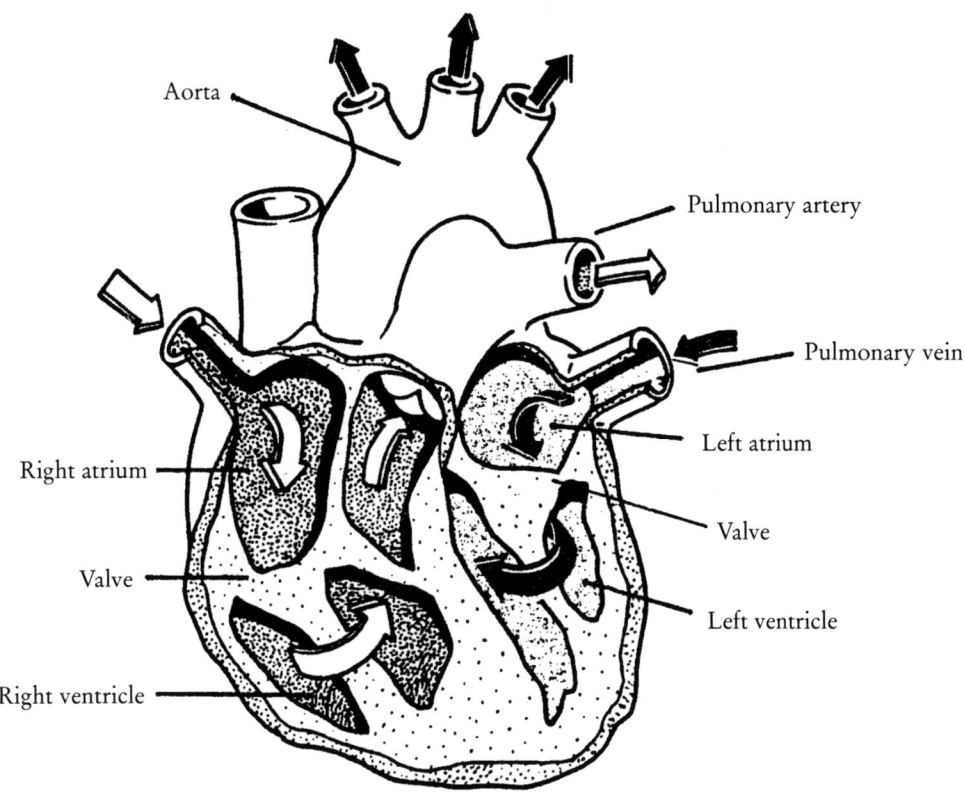

Figure 9: The heart

As the blood moves on towards the working muscles, it passes through smaller and smaller arteries with a gradual decline in pressure. By the time blood reaches the capillaries, pressure has declined to about 25 mm Hg from a starting value of about 140 mm Hg[1]. This is sufficient pressure to force about 90% of the plasma (the fluid part of the blood) through the walls of the capillary, thus delivering the essential nutrients to the working tissue and off-loading oxygen as required.

As the blood leaves the capillary to enter the venous system on its way back to the heart, it reabsorbs water from the surrounding tissue and picks up carbon dioxide, which is a waste product of muscle contraction. The carbon dioxide is then transported in the blood via the heart to the lungs for exhalation into the atmosphere.

---

1   Blood pressure is measured by the height of a column of mercury it can support. Usually it is measured just above the elbow and at rest the value is 120/80 (systolic/diastolic) millimetres (mm) of mercury (Hg). The systolic pressure in the aorta is about 140 mm Hg.

ACTIVITY 8

In the pairings given below, state which one is the higher value:

1 Blood pressure: *systolic or diastolic*

2 Force exerted on the blood: *left or right ventricle*

3 Oxygen concentration: *artery or vein*

4 Carbon dioxide concentration: *artery or vein*

Check your answers by rereading Section 2.3.

2.4 Returning Blood to the Heart

 How does the blood move back to the heart?

As it enters the small veins from the capillaries, the push given by the heart has declined to almost zero. If the blood is above the heart (for example in the head in upright posture), gravity will pull it back down, but how is the blood moved up from the hands or feet? Two mechanisms are involved.

Muscle Pump

The veins are embedded in the muscles and you will recall that they contain valves. As these surrounding muscles contract and relax, they massage the blood up the veins and the valves prevent the blood from falling back, as shown in Figure 10 on the opposite page. The system works well provided the valves are in good order. If not (as in varicose veins), some of the valves fail to seal off the tube and the blood falls back to the next healthy valve. If there are a number of faulty valves in succession, the vein will bulge (the classic indication of varicose veins).

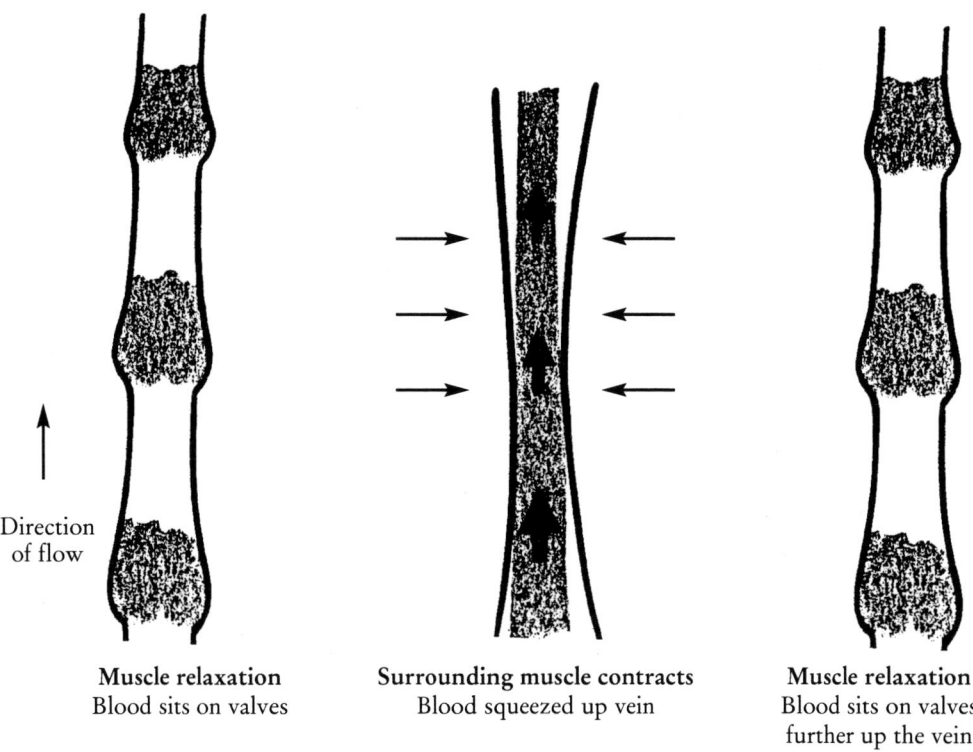

Figure 10: Moving blood up the veins

This is a very clever piece of design because it is self-regulating. At rest not very much blood is needed in the muscles, there is very little muscle activity, and consequently only a small amount of *massaging* is required. As exercise increases, more blood flows into the muscle but the muscle is contracting and relaxing more often and more forcibly, so the veins are able to move more blood back to the heart. However, this is not a foolproof system. If the muscles are not contracting and relaxing regularly, blood can pool in the extremities and this leads to a shortfall reaching the heart. With less blood being pumped by the heart, less is distributed to the brain and this may fall to below the critical level. The body's response is to faint, restoring all of the body to the same level as the heart and thus removing the problem of gravity. This is why guardsmen faint on duty, particularly when standing to attention for long periods when it is warm.

There is an important implication here for sportspeople and it explains the importance of cooling down. Exactly the same situation can occur if a performer stops immediately at the end of very intense effort (particularly in running). For a short while at the end of exercise, the cardiovascular system continues to pour vast quantities of blood into the running muscles but they have now stopped contracting. As a consequence, the blood pools in the limbs and there is a distinct possibility that the person will feel dizzy or collapse. Clearly, the best thing to do in this situation is to keep the limbs moving until the circulation has adapted to the reduction in activity (cool down thoroughly).

Thoracic (Lung) Pump

The second mechanism for returning blood to the heart is a spin-off from breathing. As mentioned before, the lungs are not able to contract. They increase and decrease in size by responding to changes in pressure in the thorax and this change in pressure is also used to *suck* blood towards the heart since the heart lies in the thoracic cavity alongside the lungs.

This **thoracic pump** which draws the blood along the veins towards the heart is caused by this pressure difference between the abdomen and the thorax. As the diaphragm is pulled down to enlarge the thoracic cavity and therefore reduce the pressure in the thorax, the pressure in the abdominal cavity is increased. This pressure gradient draws the blood up towards the heart. Again, it is a self-regulating mechanism because as the intensity of exercise increases, there is greater enlargement of the thorax to increase breathing, therefore a greater pressure difference between thorax and abdomen, and this coincides with a greater demand for blood to be returned to the heart.

2.5 Recap

The muscle requires oxygen to sustain its work for any length of time. In this chapter, we have looked at the structures responsible for delivering oxygen to the working muscle and removing the waste product, carbon dioxide. You should now feel confident to:

- describe the pathway of oxygen from the lungs to the muscles
- identify the structures which make up the oxygen transport system
- explain how the blood is moved to the working muscles and returned to the heart.

Try the following self tester to check your own understanding.

SELF TESTER 1

1 Write down the respiratory structures which form part of the oxygen transport system:

   •

   •

2 Write down the cardiovascular structures which form part of the oxygen transport system:

   •

   •

3 Explain what is meant by tidal volume:

4 Complete the following table on tidal volumes at rest and in exercise:

	Tidal Volume (Litres)	
	Rest	Maximal Exercise
Men		
Women		

Continued...

5 Explain how air is drawn into the lungs when breathing in at rest:

6 Explain why you are able to hold your breath for longer if you hyperventilate first:

7 Name five of the items carried by the blood:

-
-
-
-
-

8 Is the blood totally devoid of oxygen when it returns to the lungs?　　　　　　　　　　　　　　　　　　　Yes / No

　Explain your answer:

9 Explain how blood is moved along the:

- arteries to the capillaries:

- veins back to the heart:

Self Tester 1

1. *Write down the respiratory structures which form part of the oxygen transport system:*
   - *Airways.*
   - *Lungs.*

2. *Write down the cardiovascular structures which form part of the oxygen transport system:*
   - *Heart.*
   - *Blood-vessels.*

3. *Explain what is meant by tidal volume:*
   Tidal volume is the amount of air moving into the lungs every breath.

4. *Complete the following table on tidal volumes at rest and in exercise:*

	Tidal Volume (Litres)	
	Rest	Maximal Exercise
Men	0.5	3.0
Women	0.4–0.5	2.0

5. *Explain how air is drawn into the lungs when breathing in at rest:*
   By lowering the diaphragm to increase the size of the thorax.

6. *Explain why you are able to hold your breath for longer if you hyperventilate first:*
   Carbon dioxide is blown off, lowering the concentration in the lungs. Respiration is controlled more by changes in carbon dioxide concentration in the blood than oxygen.

7. *Name five of the items carried by the blood:*
   - *Water.*
   - *Hormones.*
   - *Fuel.*
   - *Oxygen.*
   - *Carbon dioxide.*
   - *Waste products.*
   - *Heat.*

8 *Is the blood totally devoid of oxygen when it returns to the lungs?*

No.

Explain your answer:

It is a mix of blood returning from different parts of the body, some at rest.

9 *Explain how blood is moved along the:*
- *arteries to the capillaries:*

    Pressure from the heart pushes the blood.

- *veins back to the heart:*

    By the muscle pump squeezing the veins, massaging the blood up to the next valve and on towards the heart.

If you had any difficulty, reread the relevant sections of this chapter, follow up the references, or make a note to ask a tutor, teacher, coach or friend. Other sources of help are given in the next section.

2.6 What Next?

If you would like to study further, the following texts are recommended:

Simple Texts

Fisher, AG and Jensen, CR (1990) **Scientific basis of athletic conditioning.** London, Lea & Febiger. ISBN 0-8121-1238-5. *(Out of print)*

National Coaching Foundation (1993) **The body in action.** 3rd edition. Leeds, National Coaching Foundation. ISBN 0-947850-51-1. *

National Coaching Foundation (1997) **Physiology and performance.** 3rd edition. Leeds, National Coaching Foundation. ISBN 0-947850-24-4. *

More Detailed Texts

Marieb, EN (1999) **Human anatomy and physiology.** New York, Addison Wesley, ISBN 0-20152-263-2. (Chapters 18, 19, 20 and 23)

Tortora, GJ and Anagnostakos, NP (1999) **Principles of anatomy and physiology.** New York, John Wiley. ISBN 0-47137-468-7. (Chapters 19, 20, 21 and 23)

---

* Available from Coachwise Ltd (0113 231 1310).

CHAPTER THREE
Coping with Exercise

3.0 What's in It for You?

Chapter Two showed how oxygen is transferred from the atmosphere to the working tissues, and how carbon dioxide is removed from the body. This transportation process has to speed up to meet the demands of exercise and this demand can be considerable. For example, in elite performers the amount of oxygen used in a minute can increase more than twentyfold, from about a quarter of a litre to in excess of five litres. How is this process achieved?

By the end of this chapter you should be able to:

- describe the responses in the heart, lungs and blood-vessels to a single bout of exercise
- explain the importance of oxygen transport and usage to endurance performance and to your sport
- identify the possible limiting factors in endurance performance
- take a pulse rate at rest and following exercise.

3.1 Lungs

The purpose of breathing is to maintain an adequate supply of oxygen in the alveolus so that the blood can continually be replenished, and to remove carbon dioxide as it arrives from the blood. In exercise the blood passing in the capillaries speeds up about threefold, taking approximately 0.25 seconds to pass over the alveolus. Interestingly, this matches the time it takes for oxygen to pass from the air in the alveolus to the blood, so there is potential for the blood to be fully saturated with oxygen in even the most strenuous exercise, provided that there is sufficient oxygen arriving into the alveolus.

The lungs supply oxygen to the blood more quickly in exercise in two ways:

- By increasing the surface area available for diffusion of the gases between alveoli and blood.
- By speeding up the flow of air into the alveoli.

In quiet breathing only a relatively small proportion of the lungs are being used, although all the alveoli are open because once the first breath at birth is achieved, the air sacs remain inflated. They cannot collapse because their fluid lining maintains enough surface tension to keep the walls apart. However, not all the capillary bed encasing the alveoli is open, as Figure 11 illustrates, so there is very little exchange of gases. In addition, there may be little or no movement of the air in and out of the air sac so air remains stagnant.

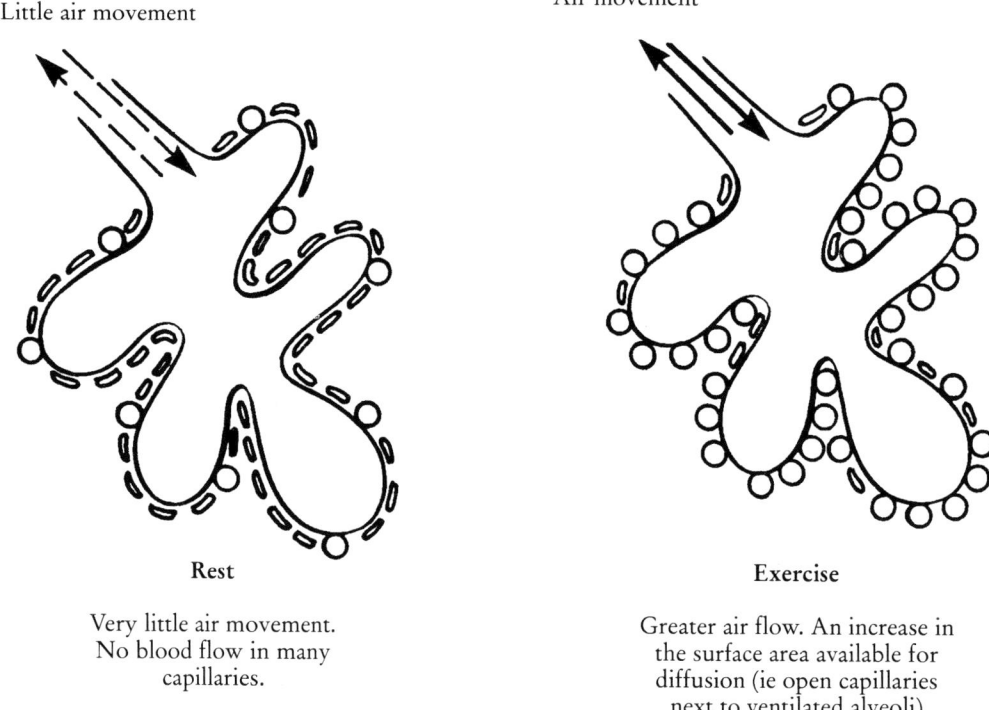

Figure 11: Alveoli surrounded by capillaries

As exercise begins, the tidal flow of air in and out of the lungs increases. Air sacs which were dormant are brought into action, atmospheric air arriving to deliver oxygen and alveolar air being washed out to the atmosphere. At the same time, more and more of the capillaries fill with blood, delivering a greater amount of blood to be replenished. The result is that a far greater volume of blood is able to pass through the lungs, and yet there is no appreciable drop in the concentration of oxygen in the blood between rest and maximal exercise (the blood is fully saturated at rest; it may be only 98% saturated in very heavy exercise but it is believed that this does not limit performance). The value of breathing oxygen-enriched mixtures is therefore questionable, although there is some evidence it may speed up recovery in damaged tissues and it clearly is of value if the oxygen content of the atmospheric air drops, as at altitude.

The next activity explains how the tidal flow to the air sacs can be increased.

ACTIVITY 9

You can carry this out yourself if you are fit and in good health. Alternatively, you can make the observations on someone else or with a sportsperson on television.

1 Observe yourself or another person at rest, sitting or preferably lying down, and then fill in the centre column of the table (at rest).

Questions	At Rest	Intense Exercise
How is air entering the body?		
Is the breathing through the nose or the mouth?		
Is the mouth open?		
What part of the torso is moving?		
Are the shoulders moving up and down?		
Is the chest moving in and out?		
How frequent is the breathing?		
Is it possible to breathe even more frequently by choice?		
At the point of maximal exertion, was the breathing rate related to the rhythm of the activity (eg running stride or pedalling speed)?		

2 Now either:
- carry out vigorous exercise such as running, cycling, stair-climbing, skipping or jumping until you are working extremely hard, and then complete the right-hand column or
- watch a sportsperson on television competing in a very demanding event (such as a middle distance running) and make these observations just as they finish the activity.

Now turn over.

It should be obvious from the previous activity that there is a very large increase in tidal volume between rest and very intense exercise. Yet even when working maximally, it is still possible to take more air into the lungs.

The table below shows typical values for tidal volume under different conditions and relates it to the maximum volume that can be expired (the vital capacity), having inspired as fully as possible first. Apart from the sex difference, the greatest influence on these values is body size and age.

Table 1: Typical values for tidal volume in young adults

	Tidal Volume (Litres)		Vital Capacity
	Rest	Max Effort	
Men untrained	0.5	3.0	5.0
Men trained	0.5	4.0	6.5
Women untrained	0.5	2.0	4.0
Women trained	0.5	3.0	5.5

This increase in tidal volume is brought about by firstly a greater depth of breathing, then by an increase in rate.

You may have noticed that the breathing rate was synchronised with the activity (for example, every second stride in running). As you can see from Figure 12, the increase in tidal volume is possible because there is a reserve of air which can be breathed in (**inspiratory reserve volume**) or breathed out (**expiratory reserve volume**). The lungs cannot be collapsed completely; there is a residual volume of about half a litre.

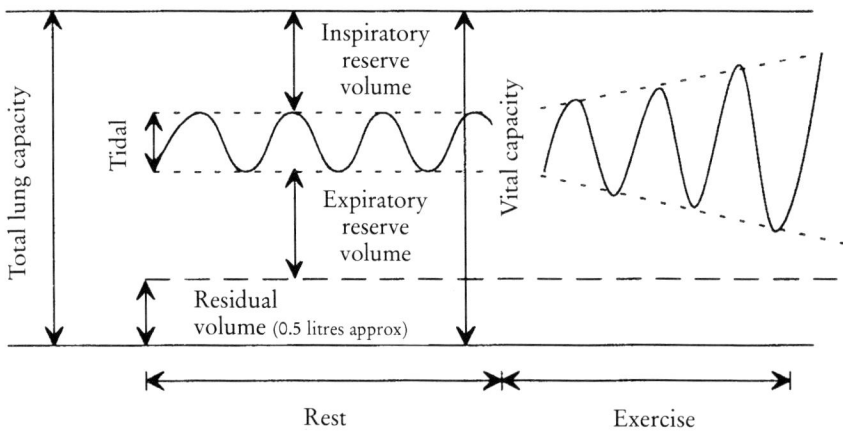

Figure 12: Lung volumes

You can check this for yourself in the next activity.

CHAPTER THREE

ACTIVITY 10

1. While sitting quietly at rest, take a normal breath and then breathe in extra air.

   Similarly, breathe out naturally and then breathe out the extra air.

   Note what happens:

   You may be surprised at the size of these reserve volumes.

2. Now repeat this during exercise. Choose an endurance activity (eg jogging or cycling).

   Note what happens:

   Now turn over.

Even when working hard at these activities, there is always a reserve. Your tidal volume never reaches your vital capacity.

The increase in depth of breathing is achieved by greater movement of the rib cage. At rest, sufficient air can be drawn into the lungs by lowering the diaphragm, but this is clearly inadequate in exercise. You should have noticed that in intense exercise the shoulders are raised and the rib cage moves outwards, considerably enlarging the thorax.

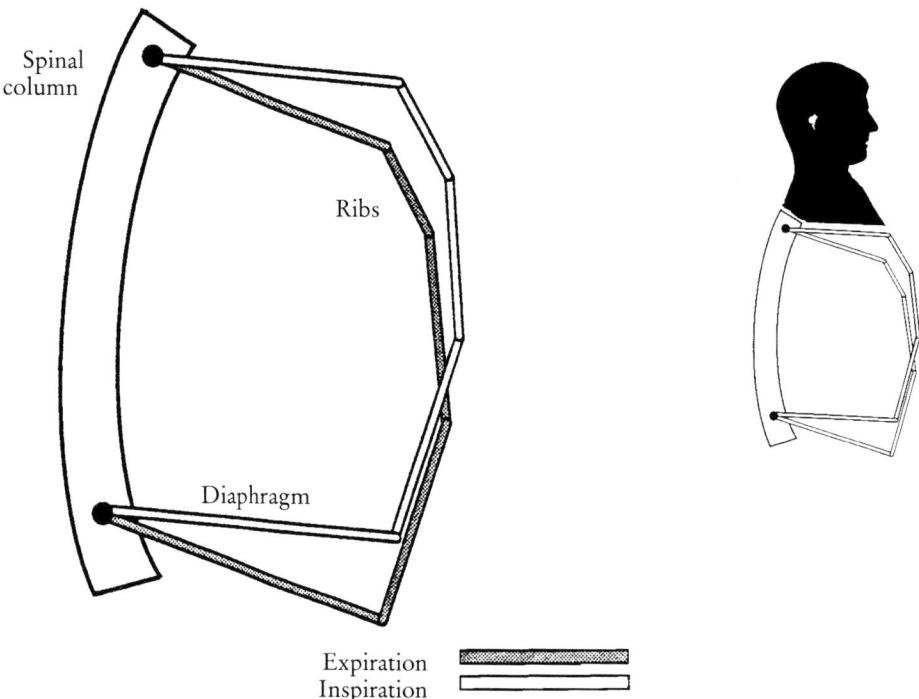

Figure 13: **Movement of the rib cage**

All this movement is achieved by the contraction of muscle – the muscles of respiration such as the intercostals lying between each of the ribs. This raises the interesting question of the oxygen demand of these muscles in relation to the muscles powering the activity.

There may be a paradox here. Does the increase in oxygen supply close to maximal work require so much extra work by the respiratory muscles that all this extra oxygen is used by them and none reaches the muscles involved in carrying out the task?

This has been suggested as one limiting factor since, in very intense exercise, about 10% of the oxygen taken up by the blood goes to fuelling the respiratory muscles.

3.2 Blood

At rest the demand for blood is quite small since only a small proportion of the body is active. Consequently, blood can be deposited in the various stores (eg in the abdomen) until the activity levels increase. At the same time, the speed at which the blood is being pushed around the system is much reduced (shown by the drop in heart rate).

The best measure of blood supply and demand is the **cardiac output,** which is the volume of blood pumped by the heart each minute. It is a product of the amount of blood pumped each beat of the heart (the **stroke volume,** sometimes called the **systolic output**) and the number of beats per minute (the **heart rate**).

? Where does the cardiac output go?

How does this distribution of blood change with exercise?

Try the next activity.

CHAPTER THREE

ACTIVITY 11

The following chart shows the cardiac output at rest (in litres per minute) and its distribution around the body. The height of the column represents the cardiac output (obviously more in exercise than at rest) and you are asked to draw in and divide up the remaining two columns proportionally to show where the blood is going as the level of exercise increases. For example, as you begin to exercise, blood is diverted from the abdomen to the working muscles to supply oxygen, and to the skin to remove heat.

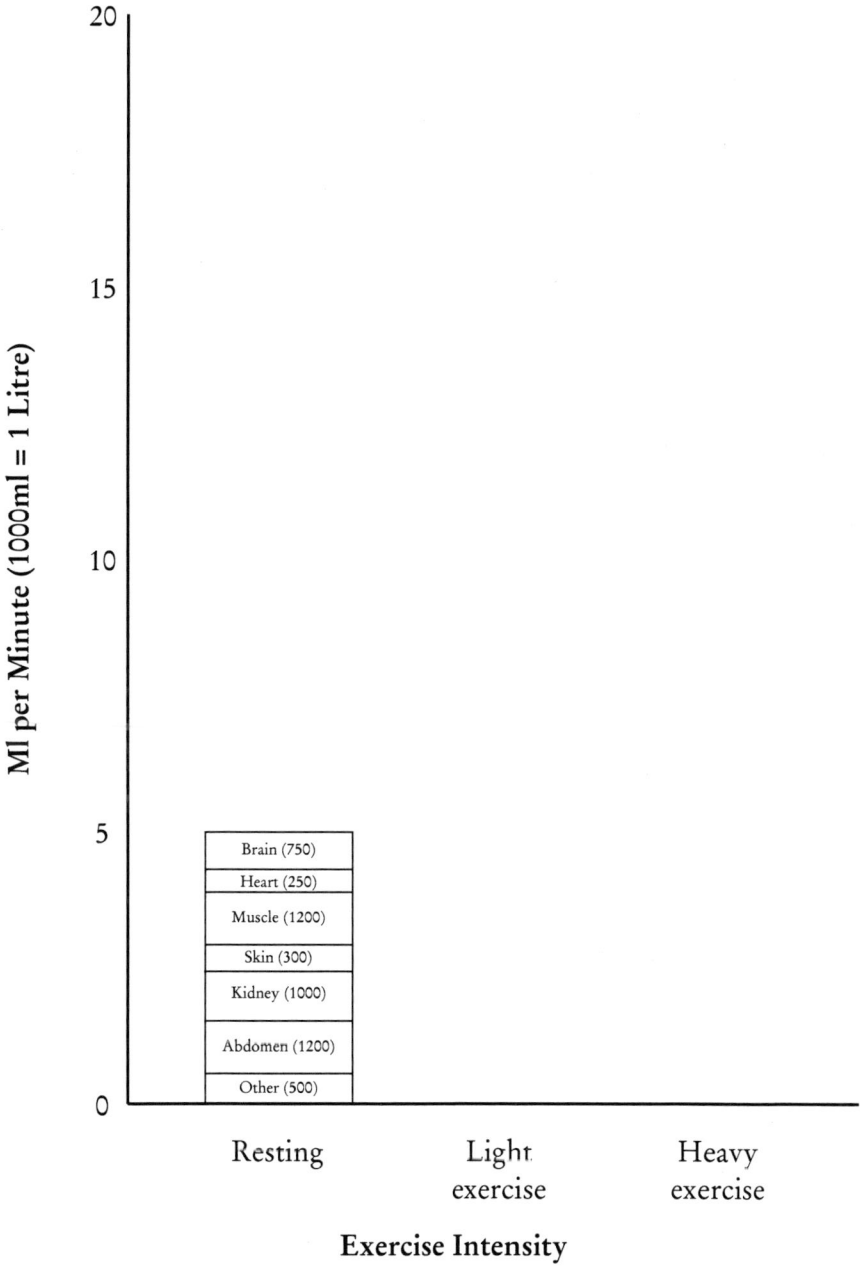

Now turn over.

*The cardiac output in light and heavy exercise will depend upon the sex, size and fitness of the individual but the figures given in the chart below are typical of a young female. More important here is the way in which the cardiac output is distributed around the body as the intensity of exercise increases. Quite obviously, there is a considerable shift in distribution towards the working muscles, with smaller increases to the heart (this muscle has to work harder too) and to the skin where heat is lost. This change in blood flow is brought about by **vasodilation** (enlargement of the tube diameter) in the arteries supplying working muscle, and **vasoconstriction** (reduction of the tube diameter) in arteries supplying other parts of the body where blood is not essential. Arteries, and the smaller arterioles, can change their diameter because they have muscle in their walls.*

The changes in blood flow to working muscle between rest and maximal exercise should not be underestimated. Cardiac output can be increased 5–7 times between rest and maximal exercise, whereas blood flow in working muscle can increase twentyfold, making an enormous difference to the amount of oxygen available.

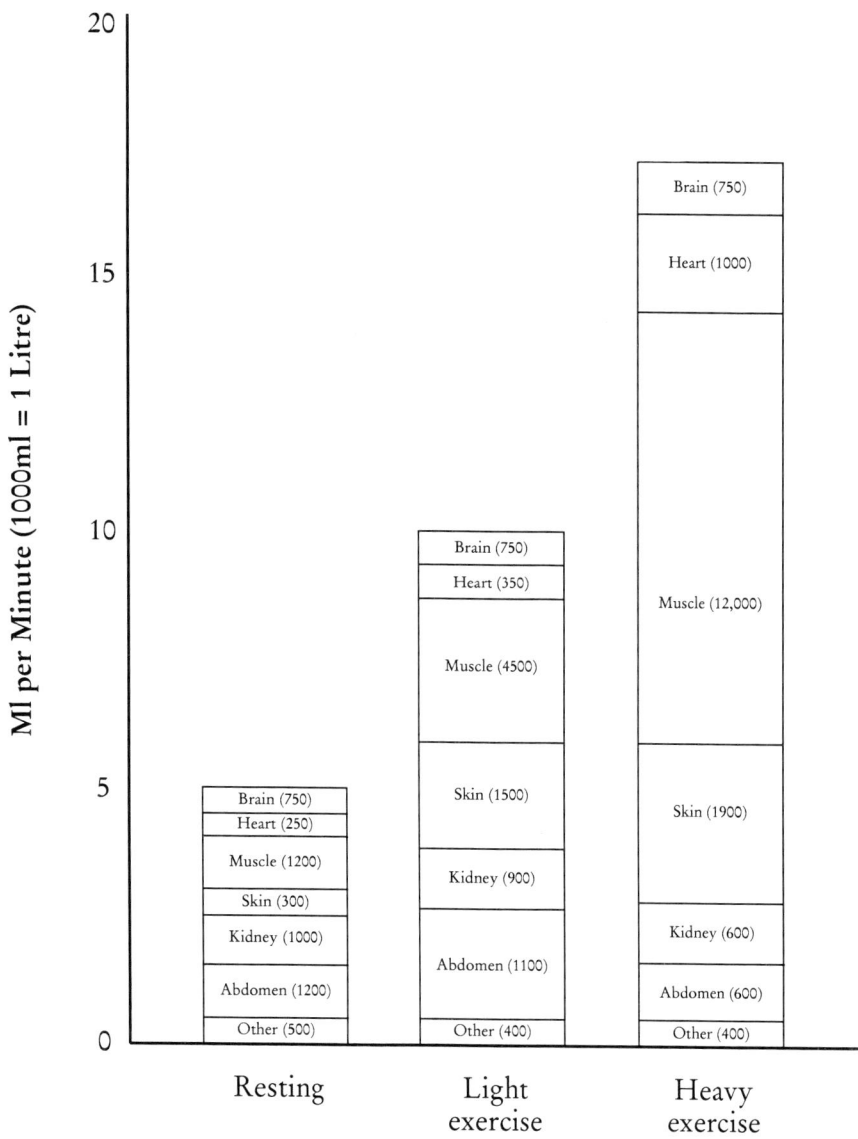

Figure 14: Blood distribution

The changes which occur in blood with exercise are not restricted to distribution and an increase in cardiac output. Obviously, this will speed up the delivery of oxygen to the working tissues, but there is another mechanism which makes a major contribution to increasing oxygen supply, and this is to do with blood chemistry.

Oxygen is carried in the blood attached to **haemoglobin,** a red pigment which makes up about one-third of the red cells. Haemoglobin will readily take up oxygen if there is plenty available, and will equally readily give it up if there is only a small amount in the surrounding tissues. Therefore, the amount of oxygen which attaches to or moves away from haemoglobin depends upon the concentration of oxygen in the surrounding environment.

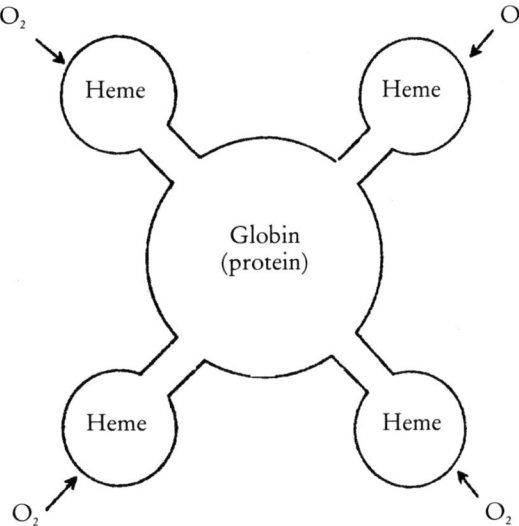

Figure 15: Haemoglobin

More precisely, the affinity of haemoglobin for oxygen depends upon the **partial pressure** of oxygen in the surrounding tissues. Partial pressure is directly related to concentration and it is necessary to understand this concept to appreciate fully oxygen delivery to muscle in exercise. This is dealt with in the following panel. If you do not wish to explore this in detail, skip to the summary on Page 52.

Partial Pressure

Imagine a box full of air. The inside of the walls of the box are being bombarded by the molecules of the gases which go to make up air, and the rate of bombardment is directly related to the concentration of the gases present. This bombardment, or pressure, prevents the box from collapsing inwards from the pressure being exerted on the outside of the box. If there is an unequal pressure on the inside and outside of the box, the box will reduce or increase in size, although the material from which the walls of the box is made will help to resist this.

Pressure on the inside walls of the box is caused by the collision of molecules, which move randomly.

Figure 16: Molecules

Pressure is a result of the collision of molecules on a surface. The outer surface of the skin is subject to the bombardment of atmospheric pressure all the time, but the nervous system is designed not to detect it consciously. In an area of lower pressure (eg altitude), body size will increase slightly, and in an area of higher pressure (eg underwater diving), the body will be squeezed to a smaller size.

What has this to do with supplying oxygen to the muscles in exercise?

The amount of oxygen which attaches or detaches to haemoglobin depends upon the partial pressure of oxygen in the surrounding tissue. Partial pressure is the pressure of each of the separate gases which make up air and their total is known as **atmospheric air pressure**. The table below shows the relative concentrations of the gases in the atmosphere and therefore their partial pressure.

Table 2: Gas concentration and partial pressure

	Gas Concentration	Partial Pressure
Total volume of air	100%	760.0 mm Hg
Nitrogen	79.03%	600.7 mm Hg
Oxygen	20.94%	159.1 mm Hg
Carbon dioxide	0.03%	0.2 mm Hg

Atmospheric pressure changes hour by hour with weather conditions but averages 760 mm Hg across the earth's surface at sea level.

If the concentration of the gases changes, then so will the partial pressures, and this is clearly the case in alveolar air. Here, there is a greater concentration of carbon dioxide and less oxygen, resulting in a partial pressure of just over 100 mm Hg for oxygen in the alveoli. Interestingly, this is just about enough pressure to ensure the haemoglobin in the blood passing by is fully saturated with oxygen (as shown in the diagram below). Even in very strenuous exercise the alveolar air maintains similar concentrations of gases because respiration successfully speeds up the delivery of atmospheric air and the removal of carbon dioxide.

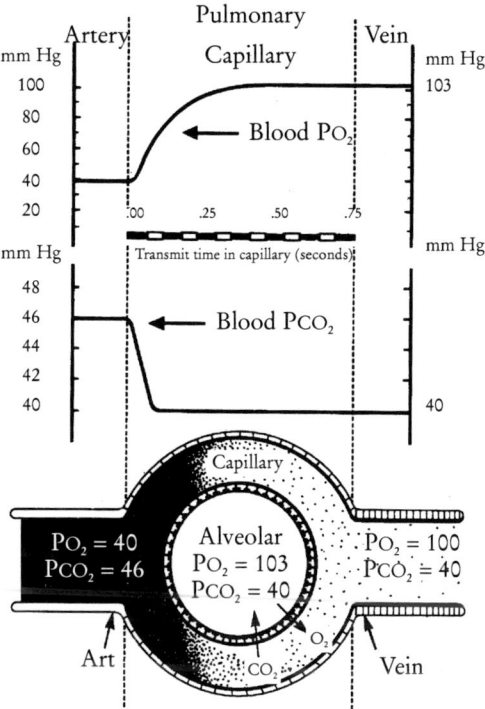

Figure 17: Capillary blood flow around alveolus

The graph on the next page (Figure 18) shows the relationship between the saturation of haemoglobin and the partial pressure of oxygen in the surrounding environment. It can be seen that at low pressures of oxygen, haemoglobin does not bind oxygen easily. As pressure increases, haemoglobin becomes much more willing to absorb oxygen, and by a partial pressure of about 100 mm Hg haemoglobin is fully saturated, although the final *topping up* is rather sluggish.

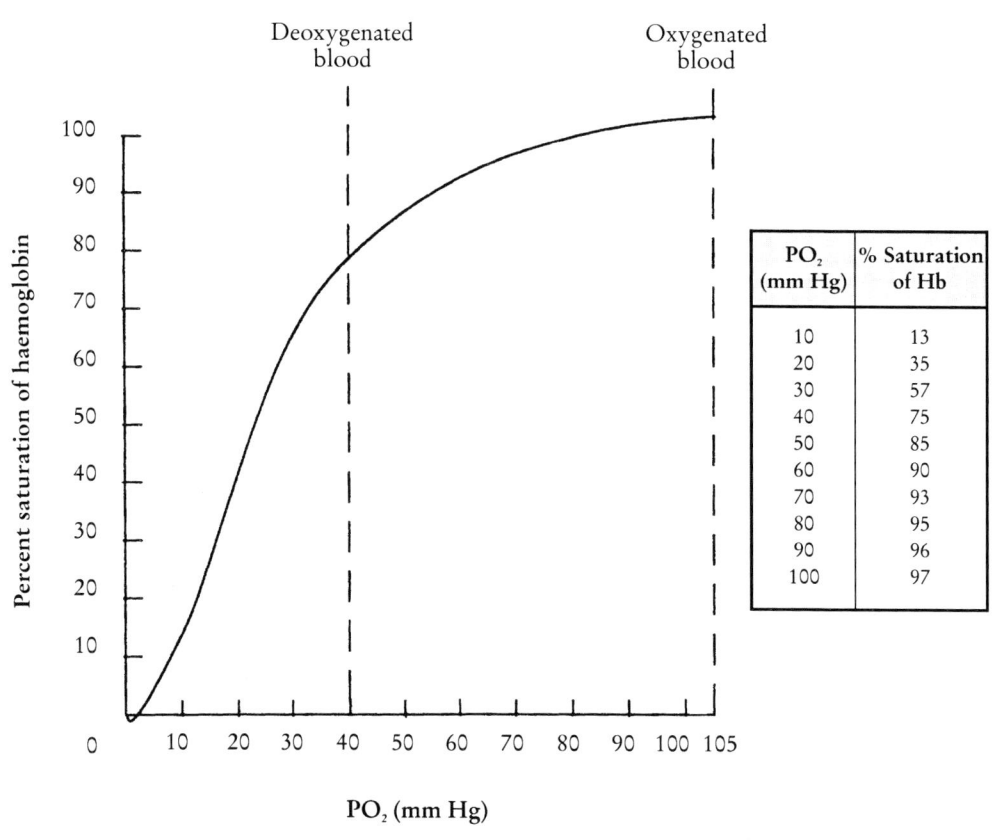

Figure 18: Oxygen dissociation curve at rest

At rest haemoglobin is fully saturated with oxygen. When it arrives at the working muscle, the partial pressure of the tissue surrounding the blood capillary will be lower than that experienced in the lungs, so oxygen will move from the haemoglobin to the muscle cells down a pressure gradient. The amount of oxygen off-loaded depends upon the steepness of this pressure gradient (in other words the partial pressure of oxygen in the muscle). At rest a typical value would be 40 mm Hg, so reducing the haemoglobin saturation to about 75% and releasing about 25% of the oxygen carried in the blood to the muscles. Clearly there is considerable potential to provide more oxygen from the blood, since only a relatively small proportion has been deposited in the working tissue, the blood returning to the heart and onwards to the lungs still containing a considerable amount of oxygen.

In exercise the working tissues are able to extract more oxygen from the haemoglobin for two reasons:

- Firstly, there is very little, if any, oxygen in the tissue surrounding the blood capillary because the working muscle is using it up, so the partial pressure of oxygen is very low and this increases the pressure gradient between haemoglobin and muscle.

- Secondly, changes brought about by exercise alter the relationship between partial pressure and haemoglobin concentration.

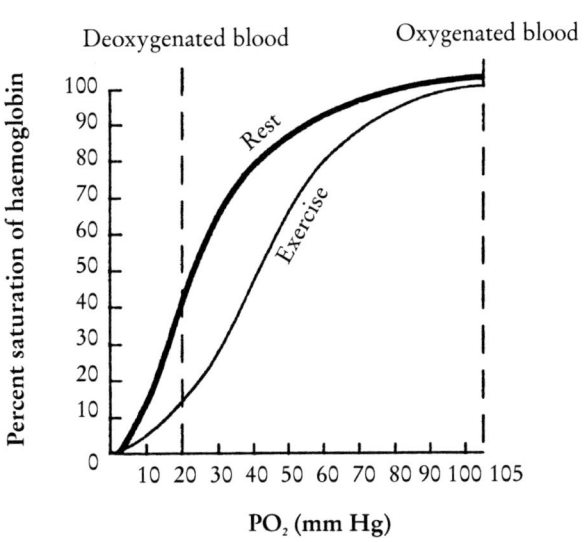

Figure 19: Oxygen dissociation curve in exercise

Figure 19 shows how the curve moves to the right, indicating that haemoglobin is less attracted to oxygen in exercise. This is mainly because exercise has produced heat and changed the acidity of the blood. Fortunately, this has very little effect on the loading of oxygen at the lungs, the drop in oxygen concentration in blood leaving the lungs being no more than 1–2%. However, the effect in the working tissue is dramatic. If the partial pressure in the working muscle in exercise was the same as at rest (40 mm Hg), haemoglobin would give up about 40% of its oxygen. Quite obviously, the partial pressure is lower than this, indeed it could fall close to zero in very intense exercise in localised parts of the muscle where there is a heavy concentration of the aerobic slow twitch fibres[1], the fibres specially designed to use oxygen to release energy for contraction. Blood leaving working muscle in heavy exercise may have given up as much as 90% of its oxygen. This blood will mix with blood returning to the lungs from other tissues, some of which will have been at rest, so the concentration of oxygen in blood arriving at the lungs is never as low as blood leaving working muscle.

It is clear that haemoglobin has a crucial bearing on aerobic performance and any attempt to increase the amount arriving at the muscle may be very beneficial. This explains interest in such practices as altitude training and blood doping since both of these will increase the concentration of haemoglobin in the blood. However, there are drawbacks, which will be explained in Section 4.3 on Page 82.

---

[1] Slow twitch muscle fibres are explained in more detail in the home study pack *An Introduction to the Structure of the Body*.

CHAPTER THREE

ACTIVITY 12

Partial pressure and its effect on oxygen supply to muscle is not an easy concept. To see how much you have understood, test yourself with the following questions:

1 Complete the following table which relates to the alveolus:

	O_2 Partial Pressure mm Hg	Haemoglobin Alveolus Saturation Percentage
At rest		
Intense exercise		

2 Using the graph of haemoglobin saturation at rest, work out the haemoglobin saturations which correspond to partial pressures of:

- 80 mm Hg

- 50 mm Hg

- 20 mm Hg

3 Explain the two reasons haemoglobin gives up more oxygen to the working muscle in exercise:

-

-

Now turn over.

1 The partial pressures at rest and in intense exercise in the alveolus are much the same, about 105 mm Hg at rest and perhaps down to 100 mm Hg in intense exercise. This results in a haemoglobin saturation of 100% at rest and about 98% saturation in intense exercise.

2 The haemoglobin saturations at rest corresponding to the partial pressures are:
- *80 mm Hg – 95%.*
- *50 mm Hg – 85%.*
- *20 mm Hg – 35%.*

3 Haemoglobin is able to release more oxygen in exercise because:
- *the amount of oxygen in the surrounding tissues is less, thus lowering the partial pressure and therefore increasing the pressure gradient from blood to muscle*
- *of changes in the blood chemistry (more heat, greater acidity).*

If you had any difficulty with these questions, reread from Page 39.

Summary

Oxygen needs a push in order for it to travel from the air in the alveolus to the blood, to the muscle capillaries and so to the muscle cell. This push is provided by the difference in pressure of oxygen – greater in the alveolus than the capillaries, greater in the muscle capillary than the muscle cell. This difference in pressure of oxygen occurs because there are differences in concentration. In exercise, changes in blood chemistry reduce the resistance to the push so more oxygen moves across.

3.3 Heart

It has been shown that in exercise there is a greater cardiac output in order to deliver more blood to the working tissues. This increase comes about for only one reason – more blood is being returned to the heart (the **venous return**), so unless blood is to back up in the system, the heart has to increase its pumping capacity. Although it takes a short while to adapt, the heart is able to do this well and can pump all of the blood returned to it. It might be thought that the pumping capacity of the heart is the limiting factor in maximal exercise, because it is unable to produce a large enough cardiac output to meet the needs of the working muscles. However, experiments have shown that it will pump all of the blood returned to it, even when the venous return is increased artificially.

This is not to say that the circulation does not limit exercise in some circumstances, but this limitation is not in the pump but in the volume of blood being circulated. It has been shown that if you can recruit in excess of 50% of your total muscle mass (which is about the quantity in the legs in a well-trained endurance performer), and work it maximally, there is not enough blood to supply sufficient oxygen. Clearly, you have to look at the demands of your sport to see if this is relevant and, if so, ensure that your training concentrates on improving blood volume and circulation.

The heart is a very effective pump, but how does it increase its output as more blood is returned to the heart? Remember that the cardiac output is dependent upon two things: the stroke volume and the heart rate. Both of these increase in exercise, stroke volume increasing by about 50% from rest to maximum work and heart rate increasing almost threefold.

Sportspeople and their coaches should be able to monitor heart rate because it is the best indicator of training intensity and recovery. In the next activity, you will be required to locate and count the pulse at rest and following exercise. The pulse is a shock wave set up by the blood surging out of the heart each beat which travels along the arteries. Study the panel over the page.

Taking the Pulse

Locating the pulse

It is commonly believed that the pulse is easy to measure but this is not so. You may be lucky and have a very distinct pulse which is easy to locate and count accurately but this is the exception rather than the rule. With practise though, you will become adept at pulse counting.

It is best to carry out this task with a partner but it is possible to do it on yourself. Do not attempt to locate the pulse at rest, rather have the person do some moderate exercise to increase cardiac output and hence the strength of the pulse. Using Figure 20 to help you, locate the pulse at the wrist (radial pulse) and then in the neck (carotid pulse). You may have to press quite hard at the base of the thumb to find the radial pulse but press only lightly in the neck. This is because the carotid pulse is carrying blood to the brain and pressing too hard may reduce the blood supply and cause dizziness. Furthermore, there is a natural reflex which slows the heart rate if you squeeze the carotid artery, and this will give a false indication of heart rate if you are trying to measure it.

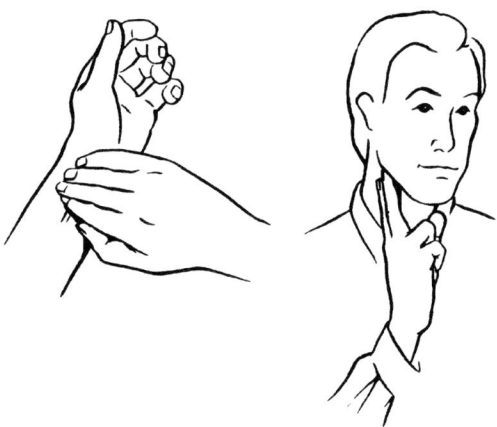

Figure 20: Locating the pulse

Counting the pulse

Practise counting the pulse rate. With your partner standing at rest, carry out a number of ten second pulse counts. The measures should be roughly similar, although there will be some fluctuation in heart rate due to body movements and psychological factors (the psychological effect can be quite large). Try asking your partner to think about an event involving strong emotions and observe the effect on the pulse rate. Your partner can help you by checking your accuracy using the other pulse location.

You are now ready to tackle the next activity.

ACTIVITY 13

You are required to take and record the pulse rate under a number of different conditions:

- Lying
- Sitting
- Standing
- Walking
- Jogging
- Stair climbing.

Sustain each condition for two minutes (except stair climbing where one minute will be sufficient).

Locate the pulse immediately and carry out a ten second count. Avoid delay after the exercise conditions, for the pulse rate will be slowing down as the person recovers and the results will be inaccurate. Inevitably it will take around 15 seconds from the end of the activity to carry out your count but it has been shown that a ten second pulse count immediately at the cessation of exercise is a reasonable estimate of exercise heart rate for most people.

Complete the table, giving the ten second pulse count and then converting it to beats per minute.

Activity	Pulse Rate in 10 Secs	Conversion to 60 Secs
Lying		
Sitting		
Standing		
Walking		
Jogging		
Stair climbing		

Now turn over.

CHAPTER THREE

You may have been surprised how much the pulse rate, and therefore the heart rate, increased with exercise. Compare your scores with the following:

- *Typical values for young adult males are given in the following table but there is a large range of normal values in the general population. Female values may be a few beats higher because they have less haemoglobin per volume of blood and therefore need to pump a little more blood to do the same amount of work.*

Activity	Endurance Trained	Untrained
Lying	40	70
Sitting	45	75

- *In untrained individuals of normal body weight, aged in their twenties, walking will elicit heart rates of about 100–130 beats per minute. These values will be higher if the individual is carrying excess weight, lower if they are trained. Obviously, speed of walking, wind conditions and slope will have an effect.*

- *Most people will subconsciously choose a jogging speed about 70–85% of their maximal heart rate, which can be estimated as 220 minus age (slightly lower in the well-trained). Consequently, if aged about twenty years, your partner will have jogged at a heart rate of 140–170 beats per minute (assuming he/she was not trying to impress you).*

It should be obvious that heart rate is very responsive to exercise and accounts for changes in the cardiac output. It might be surprising to learn that the most significant improvement in cardiac output at the start of exercise is not heart rate but stroke volume.

The more efficient physiological strategy is to increase volume before increasing rate. Consequently, stroke volume increases at the onset of exercise and reaches a maximum by the time the heart rate has increased by 50% of its potential, as the next graph shows (Figure 21). A similar situation occurs in breathing, where at the beginning of exercise tidal volume increases more rapidly than respiratory rate.

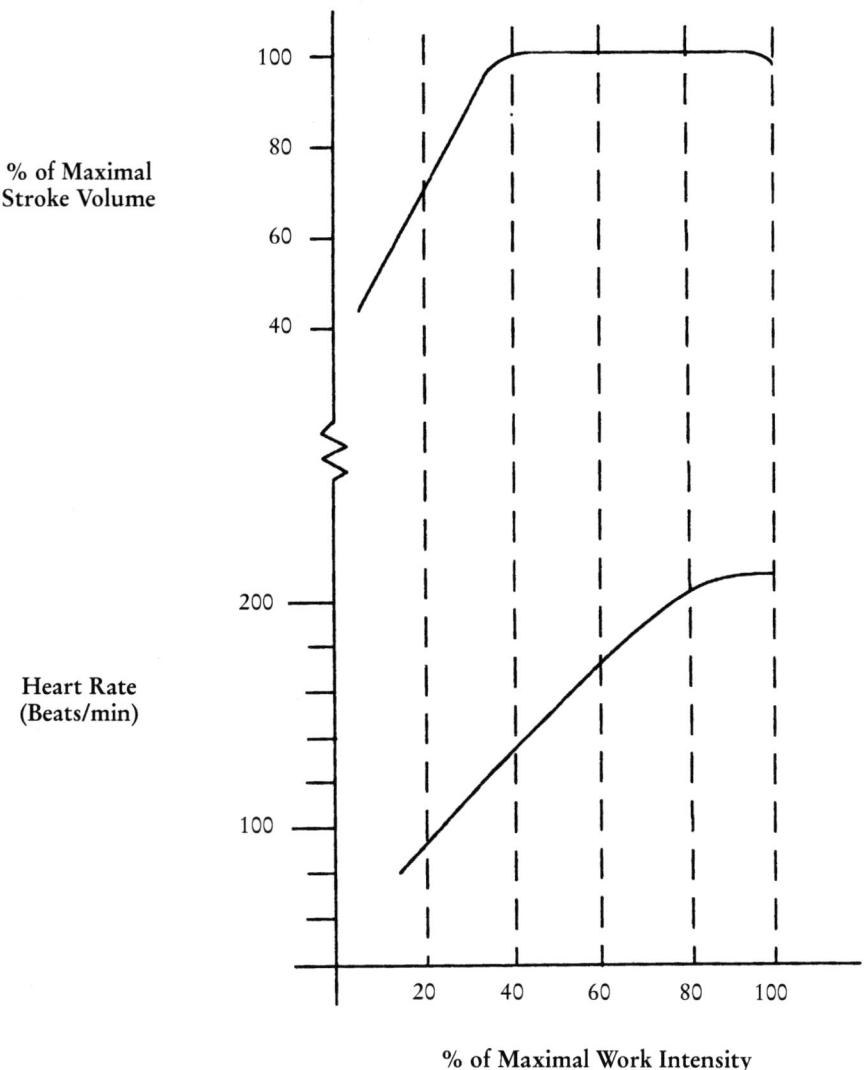

Figure 21: Stroke volume plotted against heart rate

The increase in stroke volume is brought about by an increase in the volume of the blood contained in the heart before contraction, and a greater force of contraction (a greater filling and a greater emptying). At rest not all the blood contained in the left ventricle is expelled into the aorta. As exercise intensity increases, greater emptying occurs. At the same time, more blood is arriving back at the heart to refill the ventricle during diastole, and the elastic nature of the walls allows the chamber to distend, so increasing the amount of blood in the ventricle when systole occurs.

3.4 Muscle Use of Oxygen

If you could observe the blood flowing away from a muscle, you would notice two very obvious changes between rest and exercise:

- The amount of blood flowing past would be much greater in exercise because the oxygen transport system has made the changes described earlier.
- The concentration of oxygen in this blood leaving the muscle will be less. Interestingly, there is very little difference in oxygen concentration of blood leaving heart muscle between rest and exercise, the heart relying much more on increasing flow rate. This shows how catastrophic a partial blockage of a coronary artery can be.

The muscle is clearly able to extract more oxygen and use it to release energy to do more work. So how does muscle increase its use of oxygen in exercise?

A muscle is best thought of as a collection of motor units (one nerve and all the muscle fibres it stimulates, which will vary in number depending upon the job the muscle has to do[1]). At rest there may be no motor units working at all but as the level of activity increases, more and more are recruited. The muscle is impregnated with a dense network of capillaries (see Figure 22) and these fill with blood as neighbouring muscle fibres begin to contract. As the level of activity of the muscle increases, the muscle is able to take in more and more blood.

---

1 This is explained in more detail in the NCF home study pack *An Introduction to the Structure of the Body*.

CHAPTER THREE

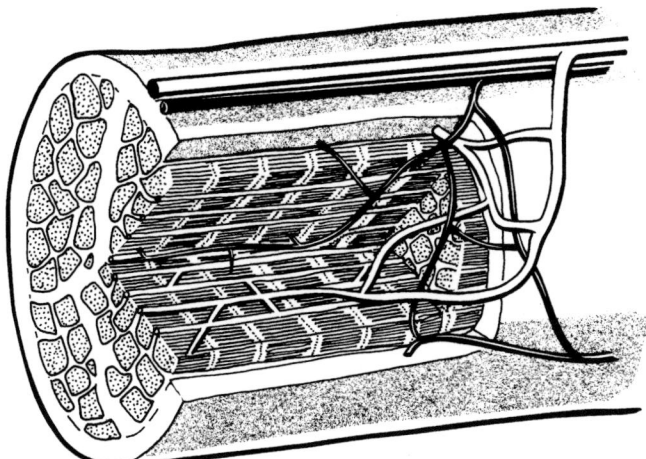

Figure 22: A section of muscle showing the dense network of blood-vessels

Obviously, the blood is rich in oxygen but the working muscle fibres in close proximity have very little. In order to equalize the concentrations, the oxygen moves out of the capillary blood and into the muscle fibres. Here it attaches to **myoglobin**, a substance very similar to haemoglobin, and is transported to the **mitochondria**, which can be regarded as the factories of the muscle, where the oxygen is used to release energy for contraction. The ability of the mitochondria to use oxygen, because of their size and number, greatly exceeds the amount of oxygen that can be delivered to the muscle fibre, so once the muscle fibre has been switched on, great demands are made upon the blood passing in the capillaries.

? Will there be any oxygen left in the blood leaving a working muscle?

The answer is yes, but it depends upon the intensity of effort. As the activity of the muscle increases, more and more motor units are recruited so more of the capillaries are close to active muscle fibres. If the exercise is sustained for long enough to allow all the capillary bed to open up, almost all of the oxygen delivered to the muscle can be taken up. It is unlikely though, that blood leaving an active muscle is ever totally without oxygen because not every capillary is ideally situated close to working fibres, and some fibres will not be working efficiently (eg because of damage). It should also be remembered that some of the muscle fibres will be **fast twitch**[1] and therefore not able to take up and use oxygen to any great extent.

---

1 Fast twitch muscle fibres are explained in more detail in the home study pack *An Introduction to the Structure of the Body.*

3.5 Recap

In this chapter, you have looked at what happens to the body during exercise and specifically the way in which oxygen is taken up by the blood in the lungs and delivered to and used by the working muscle. You should now be able to explain what is happening in the heart, lungs and blood vessels. You should also be able to consider the sort of demands on these systems imposed by your own sport and explain any limiting factors.

Check your own understanding by completing the following self tester.

SELF TESTER 2

1. State the two ways in which more oxygen is supplied to the blood as exercise increases:

    •

    •

2. Explain why it is suggested that breathing oxygen enriched mixtures may have little benefit:

3. Give one reason why breathing may:

    • not limit endurance performance:

    • limit endurance performance:

4. It is physiologically more efficient to increase volume rather than rate (ie for muscle to contract more forcibly rather than more often). Give examples of this for the:

    • lungs:

    • heart:

5 Explain why blood flow to working muscle in heavy exercise can be twenty times the resting value, yet cardiac output only increases five to sevenfold:

6 Explain why:
- blood flow to the skin increases in exercise:

- this might cause a conflict as exercise reaches a maximum:

7 Explain why more oxygen is given off by the blood to working muscle in exercise:

8 Explain why and how cardiac output is increased in exercise:

9 Suggest why blood volume rather than the pumping capacity of the heart might limit maximal endurance performance:

10 Explain in which two ways stroke volume is increased in exercise:

-

-

Now turn over.

Self Tester 2

1 State the two ways in which more oxygen is supplied to the blood as exercise increases:

- *An increase in ventilation of the alveoli (more air, and therefore oxygen, is moved in and out of the lungs).*
- *There is a greater surface area for diffusion.*

2 Explain why it is suggested that breathing oxygen enriched mixtures may have little benefit:

Because the blood is almost fully saturated (98%) with oxygen, even in very heavy exercise.

3 Give one reason why breathing may:

- *not limit endurance performance:*

    The tidal volume is only about 50% of vital capacity in maximal exercise and more air can be drawn in voluntarily.

- *limit endurance performance:*

    Close to maximal work the increase in oxygen supplied to the blood is largely used by the muscles of respiration. There is very little increase in oxygen supply to the locomotor muscles.

4 It is physiologically more efficient to increase volume rather than rate (ie for muscle to contract more forcibly rather than more often). Give examples of this for:

- *the lungs:*

    Tidal volume increases in preference to breathing rate.

- *the heart:*

    Stroke volume has reached a maximum well ahead of heart rate.

5 Explain why blood flow to working muscle in heavy exercise can be twenty times the resting value, yet cardiac output only increases 5–7 fold:

More of the blood being pumped by the heart is being diverted to the working muscle – blood is shunted to where it is needed.

6 Explain why:

- *blood flow to the skin increases in exercise:*

    Heat is being created by the contraction of muscle and has to be passed to the skin to be lost.

- *this might cause a conflict as exercise reaches a maximum:*

    Close to maximum exercise there is conflicting demand from muscle and skin. Muscle will win this battle but only for a very short time until body temperature reaches a critical value. Consequently, elite performers may appear to stop sweating when they are working very hard indeed but this level of exercise will not be sustained.

7 Explain why more oxygen is given off by the blood to working muscle in exercise:

Haemoglobin is less good at binding oxygen as heat and acidity increase in the blood; an inevitable consequence of exercise. Also, more motor units are working in the muscle so the amount of oxygen in the muscle drops, giving a greater difference in oxygen concentration between the blood and the muscle.

8 Explain why and how cardiac output is increased in exercise:

To pump the venous return (the heart pumps everything returned to it). This is achieved by an increase in both the stroke volume and the heart rate.

9 Suggest why blood volume rather than the pumping capacity of the heart might limit maximal endurance performance:

In performers working more than about 50% of their muscle mass maximally, there is not enough blood being supplied, yet the heart will pump all of the blood returned to it. It would appear that it is blood volume rather than cardiac output which may be the limiting factor.

10 Explain in which two ways stroke volume is increased in exercise:

- *By a greater filling.*
- *By a greater emptying.*

If you had any difficulty, reread the relevant sections of this chapter, follow up the references, or make a note to ask a tutor, teacher, coach or friend. Other sources of help are given in the next section.

3.6 What Next?

If you would like to study further, the following texts are recommended:

Simple Text

National Coaching Foundation (1997) **Physiology and performance.** 3rd edition. Leeds, National Coaching Foundation. ISBN 0-947850-24-4. *

More Detailed Texts

Fox, EL, Bowers, RW and Foss, ML (1988) **The physiological basis of physical education and athletics.** Dubuque, Iowa, Wm C Brown. ISBN 0-0301-1273-7. (Out of print).

Marieb, EN (1999) **Human anatomy and physiology.** New York, Addison Wesley. ISBN 0-20152-263-2. (Section 3.)

Martin, DE. and Coe, PN (1997) **Better training for distance runners.** Champaign IL, Human Kinetics. ISBN 0-8801-1530-0. (Chapter 3.)

* Available from Coachwise Ltd (0113 231 1310).

CHAPTER THREE

CHAPTER FOUR
Training Oxygen Transport and Utilisation

4.0 What's in It for You?

The purpose of training is to reduce the stress on the body imposed by exercise, so that any level of work can be carried out more comfortably and there is an increase in the maximum amount of work that can be achieved. If the oxygen transport system is trained, it is able to sustain sub-maximal work like jogging or recreational cycling for longer, cover more distance in the same time, or complete a set distance such as a race more quickly.

This chapter will help you to design successful aerobic training programmes for your sport and understand more clearly the adaptations which take place in the oxygen transport system as a result of that training. In particular, by the end of the chapter you should be able to:

- explain the principles of training and especially how they relate to aerobic training
- explain what is meant by aerobic and anaerobic thresholds
- assess the aerobic demands of your sport
- explain why aerobic training is useful for all sports
- design an aerobic training programme for your sport
- explain the effects of aerobic training
- explain the structural and functional changes in the heart, lungs and circulation as a consequence of training.

4.1 Principles of Training

This section builds on the information on training principles in *The Body in Action*[1] and relates it to aerobic training. Start checking your knowledge by completing the following activity.

1 NCF Introductory Study Pack available from Coachwise Ltd (0113 231 1310).

ACTIVITY 14

1 Explain what is meant by:

- aerobic:

- anaerobic:

2 List and briefly explain as many principles of training as you can:

Training Principle	Explanation

3 Highlight those that you feel are particularly pertinent to aerobic training.

Now turn over.

CHAPTER FOUR

1. • *Aerobic means **in the presence of oxygen** and therefore aerobic training is any in which the oxygen transport system is supplying all of the oxygen needed to do the work.*
   • *Anaerobic means **without oxygen**. In anaerobic training the body is working so hard that all of the oxygen needed cannot be supplied by the oxygen transport system.*

2. *The following table provides a list of training principles. Do not worry if you have not used precisely the same terms as long as the meaning is the same. The table is based on the principles discussed in The Body in Action.*

Training Principle	Explanation
Individual differences	Individuals will respond differently to the same training.
Adaptation	Changes take place in the body as it adapts to the demands imposed by training.
Overload	The body must be subjected to increased physical stress to improve its condition. The three overload factors are frequency, intensity and time.
Progression	Increase the training load slowly.
Specificity	Training effects are specific, so the training must be appropriate to the sport requirements.
Variation	Avoid boredom by varying training routines.
Long-term planning	Training effects take time and must be planned.
Reversibility	Training effects are quickly lost if training stops.
Recovery	Ensuring sufficient time is given to allow the body to recover from the stress of training.

If you had any difficulty, you are advised to read the relevant section in The Body in Action before continuing.

The principles of training apply to all forms of training but some are more important than others depending upon the adaptations required. With regard to aerobic training, the key elements are overload, progression, recovery[1] and specificity. Before looking at general principles, it is important to examine the specific aerobic demands of your sport.

---

1 You will find this under individual differences in *The Body in Action*.

ACTIVITY 15

Answer the following statements by placing a circle around the most accurate response:

Sport:

While participating in my sport:

- I am out of breath   Often   Sometimes   Rarely
- there are long periods of time when I am aware of my breathing   Often   Sometimes   Rarely
- during training practices, I stop to catch my breath   Often   Sometimes   Rarely
- there are short periods of very hard work followed by rest intervals   Often   Sometimes   Rarely

Now turn over.

If you answered **often** to the first two questions, you are likely to be involved in a high endurance aerobic sport. In the last question, an answer of **often** may indicate that there is an important aerobic basis to your sport, although it also has anaerobic demands. This is very likely to be the case if you answered **often** to the third question.

If most of your answers were **rarely,** it is likely that aerobic endurance is not very important, although remember that research suggests that by improving your aerobic fitness, you are likely to improve concentration. Therefore, if your sport places high demands on concentration over a long period of time (eg archery, golf), aerobic fitness will be advantageous.

4.2 Key Principles for Aerobic Training

Having considered the aerobic demands of your sport, you should be able to answer the question *How important is this type of training for my sport?* This will help you design a good aerobic training programme using the principles of training outlined below:

- Overload (intensity, duration and frequency).
- Progression.
- Recovery.
- Specificity.

Overload

It is important to realise that the body is dynamic not static. It will respond to the stresses put upon it by the environment. If you do more exercise, the body will lay down more tissue (muscle, connective tissue such as tendon or bone), to cope with that exercise. If activity is reduced, the body will remove tissue. This assumes your diet is adjusted accordingly, otherwise tissue will be lost due to a drop in exercise but you may be laying down so much fat that your body weight either remains constant or increases. To stimulate the laying down of new tissue, the body has to be exposed to repeated bouts of exercise which overload the system. This principle of overload is fundamental to training and can be brought about by increasing the intensity, duration or frequency of exercise.

Intensity is by far the most important aspect of aerobic training and has been quite well researched in relation to aerobic conditioning for health. It is now generally accepted that there is an aerobic threshold below which there is insufficient stimulus to the cardiovascular system to bring about any long-term changes. This threshold occurs at different heart rates for different people and varies with age and fitness but a general value of 60% of maximal heart rate is reasonable[1].

---

1 Remember that maximal heart rate is affected by age and is roughly estimated to be 220 minus age.

Equally, there is an upper limit above which the body can no longer sustain aerobic exercise, has to recruit anaerobic resources, and therefore will fatigue quickly. This **anaerobic threshold** also depends upon age and fitness but can be regarded as no greater than 90% of maximal heart rate, and may be much less in untrained people.

Remember, aerobic training is training in which the oxygen transport system is supplying all the oxygen needed to do the work. In anaerobic training, the body is working so hard that all the oxygen needed cannot be supplied by the oxygen transport system. Note that oxygen is present but there is just not enough of it. If work is to continue, it is necessary to recruit the fast twitch muscle fibres[1], which can release energy without needing oxygen. In this situation the body can build up an oxygen deficit, but there will come a point when no more deficit can be tolerated and the performer has to stop or slow down so the debt can be repaid. The point where the deficit starts to build up is described as the anaerobic threshold.

ACTIVITY 16

To check you have grasped these concepts, indicate which of the following activities are aerobic and which are at least partly anaerobic:

- Jogging: Aerobic / Anaerobic
- 400m running: Aerobic / Anaerobic
- Windsurfing: Aerobic / Anaerobic
- Boxing: Aerobic / Anaerobic
- Motor racing: Aerobic / Anaerobic

Now turn over.

---

[1] This is discussed in more detail in the NCF home study pack *An Introduction to the Structure of the Body*.

This may appear to be quite an easy task. If you adopt the criteria that an aerobic activity is one which can be carried out for a long period of time, and anaerobic exercise cannot be sustained for very long without a rest interval:

- *Jogging*　　　　　　　*Aerobic*
- *400m running*　　　　*Anaerobic*
- *Windsurfing*　　　　　*Aerobic*
- *Boxing*　　　　　　　*Anaerobic*
- *Motor racing*　　　　 *Aerobic*

In general, this is true but both aerobic and anaerobic work play a part in each of the activities to a greater or lesser degree.

At the highest level, 400m runners may be working above their anaerobic threshold for all the race, but in boxing there may be long periods of low intensity work with spasmodic bursts of high activity. In jogging there will be hills to climb, windsurfers may be working anaerobically with their arms to fight the wind in gusty conditions, and motor racing drivers have to brace themselves against large forces when cornering.

It is important to realise that the recommendations described earlier relate to training the slow twitch muscle fibres. Certainly, there may be occasions when you want to train the slow twitch fibres (eg when recovering from injury, or at the beginning of the off-season training programme) but if you are working with serious sports performers, their slow twitch fibres should already be well trained. Therefore for sport, aerobic training needs to be intense enough to switch on the fast twitch fibres to develop their aerobic potential, although this is more limited.

It should be apparent that there are two intensities at which to train to improve aerobic endurance:

- **Low intensity exercise** is required to train the slow twitch fibres and this is the basis of the recommendations for improving aerobic endurance for health
(eg to reduce the risk of coronary artery disease).

- Endurance performers require greater aerobic endurance and therefore need **high intensity training** to improve the aerobic capacity of the fast twitch fibres, especially the fast oxidative fibres which have the ability to make a significant aerobic contribution.

Aerobically training the fast twitch fibres can be achieved in two ways:

- Exercising at or just below the anaerobic threshold will have this effect but the difficulty is knowing where the anaerobic threshold lies. The most common method of assessing anaerobic threshold is to measure **blood lactate** to obtain the onset of blood lactate accumulation, which indicates that the supply of oxygen is insufficient and anaerobic metabolism is being used to meet the shortfall. Other techniques possible are measuring lung ventilation (the **ventilatory threshold**) or heart rate (the heart rate break away point) but the techniques to do these measurements are not well developed and not all people show these features.
- The second method of aerobically training the fast twitch fibres is to exercise at a somewhat lower intensity, but still well above the aerobic threshold for a long time. Here, fatigue will begin to set in, exhausting slow twitch fibres and therefore needing the fast twitch fibres to help to sustain the same level of work.

As with intensity, the **duration** of the training session depends upon the fitness level of the individual and the reasons for the training. Those individuals interested only in improving their health-related fitness, and therefore doing low intensity training, should follow the guidelines of the American College of Sports Medicine[1]. Of more interest here is the recommendation for endurance performers, which is higher intensity training aimed at improving the aerobic capacity of the fast twitch fibres.

The optimum duration of one aerobic training session depends upon the training intensity. It has been shown that training at or just below the anaerobic threshold has to be maintained for at least 15 minutes to be effective but the training effect diminishes rapidly beyond 35 minutes. The theoretical explanation of these values is not well understood, but it may be more to do with the level of training of the performer used in the research rather than any critical physiological events. Most well trained individuals can sustain 15 minutes of high intensity aerobic work so little, if any, adaptation will take place if the duration of training is less. Equally, few individuals will be able to sustain more than 35 minutes of continuous exercise at this level without fatigue, with a consequent drop in intensity and therefore less training effect.

An alternative method is to train at a somewhat lower intensity (but still high intensity training). For this to be effective a longer duration of training is required. It has been shown that if training intensity is less than 90% of maximum heart rate (the anaerobic threshold of a well trained endurance performer is likely to be about 90% of maximum heart rate), the training has to be sustained for more than 35 minutes.

---

[1] This can be found in the American College of Sports Medicine (1991) *Guidelines for exercise testing and prescription.* Philadelphia, Lea & Febiger. ISBN 0-8121-1324-1.

CHAPTER FOUR

Clearly, a choice has to be made between these two strategies and current fitness status should be taken into account. The duration of the event will be an important consideration, and will influence the weighting of aerobic training between the two alternatives. If the event is relatively short, such as team games or racket games, most of the training should be at the anaerobic threshold. In longer events, training at just below the anaerobic threshold is appropriate. It has been shown in middle distance running that this higher intensity training should comprise about 15% of the total aerobic training time in pre-season training, rising to about 25% of this time during the season.

ACTIVITY 17

To test your understanding of training intensity and duration, place the following in the appropriate part of the table according to where they would do most of their training:

- Jogger for health.
- 1500m athlete.
- Recreational jogger entered for half marathon.
- Elite club athlete training for ten mile road race.

		Duration	
		15–35 mins	Longer than 35 mins
Low Intensity			
High Intensity	Below anaerobic threshold		
	At anaerobic threshold		

Now turn over.

Check your answer with the following:

		Duration	
		15–35 mins	Longer than 35 mins
Low Intensity		Jogger for health	Jogger for half marathon
High Intensity	Below anaerobic threshold		Road racer
	At anaerobic threshold	1500 metre runner	

Both joggers (for health and for half marathon) would be doing low intensity training, with the one entered for the half marathon doing the longer duration. Occasionally, of course, this individual may train at a higher intensity to try to improve overall time but this would be only a small part of the training programme. The 1500m race is of short duration but good aerobic fitness is essential so this athlete would train at the anaerobic threshold. The elite club athlete, who would be competing over much longer distances, would do some of this type of training but most of the aerobic training programme would be devoted to high intensity running at below the anaerobic threshold. Some long, low intensity runs would also be carried out, mainly off-season.

The **frequency** of training depends upon the current fitness of the individual. Training twice a week will be beneficial for those with a maximal oxygen uptake of less than 45 ml/min/kg[1] in women, 50 ml/min/kg for men. However, this level of aerobic fitness, although good for the general population, would only be encountered in poorly trained endurance sportspeople or those returning after a long injury or lay-off.

It has been suggested that the optimum frequency of aerobic training is four times a week. Certainly, this will have beneficial effects for many sportspeople but there are individuals already training more often than this. It is important to realise that this recommendation relates to the intensity and duration of training described before, and those currently training more often may be doing poor quality work and therefore receiving little benefit. Nevertheless for some individuals, training more than four times a week may be necessary to bring about improvement. You will have to decide what is most appropriate for yourself or your performer.

1 **Maximal oxygen uptake** is a measure of the maximal amount of oxygen being consumed, and this occurs close to maximal work. To allow comparison between individuals of different sizes, it is expressed as a volume (millilitres) per minute in relation to a kilogram of body weight (ie ml/min/kg).

Progression

A sportsperson undertaking the training programme outlined earlier will show considerable improvement, but this improvement will tail off with time as the body adapts to the stress imposed. Since the body is dynamic, the overload has to be progressively increased (progressive overload) if continuous improvement is sought, otherwise performance will plateau once the body has adapted to the initial increase in workload.

Progression can be brought about by increasing any one of the three elements since this will produce more work for the performer, but it is important to keep in mind the nature of the sport or event. There is little point in increasing the duration of training if it already exceeds the duration of the event by a considerable margin, and the frequency of training sessions has to take into account the whole lifestyle of the performer. Most importantly, it has been seen that intensity is the key to overload.

After a short period of training, the body will have adapted so that the original intensity no longer imposes the same stress. For example, if the individual had been training at the onset of blood lactate accumulation, this will no longer be the case and a further assessment would have to be made to obtain the new, higher level of work. In this way, the body continues to be stressed and will respond by further adaptation.

In the next activity, you will be encouraged to analyse your own or your performer's current training programme in light of the guidelines offered on progression.

ACTIVITY 18

1 Within the same block of training (eg during off-season training), examine the training diary for two separate weeks about four weeks apart. Write down any increases in:

- intensity (is the performer working harder?)

- duration (is the total training time for the week more?)

- frequency (are there more sessions per week?)

2 Comment on the effectiveness of the training programme in terms of progression:

Now turn over.

An increase in any of these factors shows progression but remember that the most important factor is intensity. Be wary of an increase in only duration or frequency. For performance to improve, there must be an improvement in quality as well as quantity.

This is not a simple issue. At some times in the year, progression may be achieved by reducing quantity and increasing quality (eg at the beginning of the competitive programme). You will need to decide the criteria for progression and then examine the training diary to see if it is happening.

Recovery

It is extremely important to recognise the value of recovery. The effect of training is to destroy tissue and there will be little or no adaptation if training occurs every day.

Recovery does not necessarily mean rest. It is better to think of two types of recovery:

- **Active recovery** is a low intensity, short duration training session which helps the repair and rebuilding mechanisms and speeds up the refuelling of the energy stores. It should be done, for example, the day after a tiring race or as part of a cycle of heavy training.
- **Rest recovery** is important prior to competition to ensure the energy stores are full. A current suggestion is that including some very low level exercise may help to speed up energy storage if carried out in combination with carbohydrate loading[1].

Providing the body is given time to recover, the body lays down new tissue in slightly greater quantities than the tissue destroyed in response to training. Consequently, every training programme should highlight the recovery days and ensure they occur at frequent intervals – preferably more often than once per week. It is suggested that a mixture of active and rest recovery days is important if injury and staleness are to be avoided, but as yet there is no evidence to support this recommendation.

1   This is a technique used by some endurance performers to trick the body into storing more energy than normal.

Are your performers getting enough recovery? Try the next activity.

ACTIVITY 19

If you are in serious training, you may wish to carry out this exercise on yourself. If not, ask one of your performers or a committed performer in your sport.

1. Obtain the training diary for the last four weeks (if your performer does not have one, either compile one from memory or ask the performer to keep one for the next four weeks. Do not explain why you want the information until afterwards).

2. Examine the diary carefully and identify any periods of 24 hours or longer when the performer was recovering.

3. Work out the work-day to recovery-day ratio, and the longest continuous number of days without a recovery day.

4. Log your findings and comment on whether or not the performer is giving sufficient time to recovery:

Now turn over.

There should be a period of at least 24 hours every 4–7 days when there is no training. Remember, active recovery is not training.

The problem is how to fit everything into the training programme. It may be better to train two or three times a day (build up to it gradually), with recovery days every three or four days, than to train once a day every day, providing the type of training is varied.

Specificity

It is self-evident that the training programme should fit precisely the physiological demands of your sport, as far as they are known. Obviously, you will have decided before beginning to design your programme to what extent aerobic fitness is important (refer back to Activity 15 on Page 63). It is essential that the volume of aerobic training is in balance with the demands of the sport and allows for other types of training.

Another issue of fundamental importance is that the adaptations resulting from aerobic conditioning are specific not only to the cardiovascular system but also to aerobic aspects of muscle. A running programme will produce training effects specific to running, a cycling programme to cycling, and so on. There are general benefits to the heart, lungs and blood-vessels but it is essential that the focus of training is on those muscles responsible for the sport-specific movements if the full benefits of aerobic training are to be achieved. The old adage *the best training for my sport is my sport* is true, provided the training is stressful enough to overload the body, and this is not always possible because of the nature of some sports. It may not be possible, for example, in sports with a high skill level (eg tennis) and in team games where a player's contribution may vary considerably between games.

Why do aerobic training?

Aerobic training is part of almost every sport but it is important to understand the reasons why it is included to ensure it is carried out effectively. There are three reasons to train aerobically:

- Aerobic endurance is a fundamental part of the sport. It is part of the training for the event.
- It is necessary to improve aerobic fitness so that other types of training are successful. For example, a 200m runner may quit in his sprint training because heart and lungs are fatigued and before the legs are full stressed.
- As part of active recovery.

CHAPTER FOUR

ACTIVITY 20

Decide whether or not aerobic training is necessary for the following activities and give your reasons. An example is provided for you:

Sport	Aerobic Training	Reason
Field hockey	Yes	Fundamental part, base for other training, active recovery.
Marathon running		
Snooker		
Sprint cycling		
Fencing		
Rock climbing		
Your sport:		

Now turn over.

Check your answers with the following table:

Sport	Aerobic Training	Reason
Field hockey	Yes	Fundamental part, base for other training, active recovery.
Marathon running	Yes	Fundamental, active recovery especially after long training runs and races.
Snooker	Yes	No great demands on aerobic endurance but improve concentration.
Sprint cycling	Yes	Good aerobic base for other training, active recovery after competition.
Fencing	Yes	Good aerobic base for other training, active recovery after competition.
Rock climbing	Yes	Active recovery during periods of intense weight training (strength and endurance).
Your sport:	Yes / No?	

You will probably be able to establish the correct answer for your own sport by comparing your sport with the examples provided. If not, or to check your answer, ask a senior coach, tutor or teacher.

You should now have enough information to design an aerobic training programme for your sport. The next activity will help you.

ACTIVITY 21

Using your own sport (or one which you know something about and has aerobic demands if your sport is not aerobic), analyse the different physiological demands and then design a suitable programme:

Sport:

1. Movement analysis:

   Think through the requirements of your sport carefully and then provide the following information:

   - Identify the important components of fitness (eg aerobic, strength, speed) and rank the importance of each by placing a 1 beside the most important, 2 beside the next and so on:

Component	Ranking

   - Identify the form of locomotion (eg running, cycling) and if more than one, rank them in importance:

Form of Location	Ranking

   - State the purpose/s of aerobic training:
     - Active recovery   Yes / No
     - Base for other training   Yes / No
     - Essential part   Yes / No

Continued...

CHAPTER FOUR

2 Designing the programme:

Using the information from Question 1, design a suitable four week aerobic programme for off-season training. Ensure you include sufficient detail about the intensity and duration for each of the training sessions. Use the following sheets if they are useful:

Week One:

Monday	
Tuesday	
Wednesday	
Thursday	
Friday	
Saturday	
Sunday	

CHAPTER FOUR

Week Two:

Monday	
Tuesday	
Wednesday	
Thursday	
Friday	
Saturday	
Sunday	

Continued...

CHAPTER FOUR

Week Three:

Monday	
Tuesday	
Wednesday	
Thursday	
Friday	
Saturday	
Sunday	

―――― CHAPTER FOUR ――――

Week Four:

Monday	
Tuesday	
Wednesday	
Thursday	
Friday	
Saturday	
Sunday	

Now turn over.

Check if:

- *your programme meets the specifications you identified in your movement analysis*
- *the volume of training is reasonable in relation to the relative importance of aerobic fitness to your sport*
- *there is progression from week to week and examine both the weekly duration of training and the training intensity*
- *there is sufficient recovery.*

Obviously there are no right and wrong answers. The guidelines must be adapted to meet the individual needs of your performer. If you are not sure how successfully you have carried out this task, discuss your programme design with a coach, teacher or tutor.

4.3 Adaptations with Aerobic Training

The purpose of training is to bring about adaptations in the body which are beneficial to performance. Physically, the individual will become a different person. If you were to carry out the training programme you have devised, what long-term structural and functional changes would you hope to see?

There are several outcomes of aerobic training but the most significant functional changes are as follows:

- The same amount of oxygen can be delivered with less physiological stress. Although the amount of oxygen needed to carry out the task may not have changed (eg it requires the same amount of oxygen to run at 10 kph on the flat before and after training[1]), the body can deliver it to the working muscles more effectively. The same task feels much easier to perform after training.

- The maximum amount of oxygen which the body can deliver to the working tissues is greater after training. Consequently, the maximum amount of work the body can do aerobically increases with training.

---

[1] This is not strictly true but it is almost true. With training you may become more skilful at the task so you can do it with slightly less muscle mass and therefore less oxygen. This is what is meant by **running economy**.

These improvements in performance arise from changes in the lungs, heart, blood-vessels, and in the muscles themselves.

Lungs

Adaptations in the lungs produce improvements in both ventilation of the alveoli and diffusion between alveolus and blood.

The capacity of the lungs increases due to greater elasticity of the air sacs and stronger respiratory muscles. Little effect is seen at rest but in moderate exercise there is a reduction in breathing rate and an increase in tidal volume. The oxygen cost of breathing is also reduced. The volume of air moved in and out of the lungs at rest is much the same before and after training but there is a marked improvement in the maximum volume that can be moved. Well trained endurance performers are able to improve their maximum minute volume (volume of air expired per minute) by as much as 40% above their untrained state.

All of this ensures the alveoli receive sufficient oxygen to meet the improved diffusion rate between alveolus and blood, and the greater volume of carbon dioxide moving from blood to alveolus is expelled from the body. The increased diffusion rate is brought about by a larger surface area for diffusion and a greater partial pressure difference between alveolus and venous blood, because the working muscles have extracted more oxygen from the blood. How they are able to do this will be explained later.

Heart

The heart can be regarded as a muscle pump and, like any muscle, it responds readily to training. The trained heart is both larger and stronger, producing a greater cardiac output. At rest, the cardiac output is about five litres per minute in both the trained and untrained. During sub-maximal work, the cardiac output is less in the well trained because the muscles are able to make more efficient use of the blood pumped by the heart.

Most of the adaptations with training relate to stroke volume. The greater venous return to the heart (resulting from a more effective muscle and thoracic pump) stimulates an increase in the size of the heart chambers and greater stretching of the walls. As a consequence, more blood can enter the heart. At the same time, the walls of the heart thicken as more muscle tissue is laid down and this produces a greater force of contraction. The outcome of all this is an increase of up to 50% in maximum stroke volume with training.

Since the trained heart is larger, the heart will choose to beat less often with a larger stroke volume. Consequently, heart rate at rest and in sub-maximal work will be lower. This is why heart rate is used as a measure of training status – the fitter the individual the lower the heart rate for a given amount of work. There may be a small reduction, perhaps 2–5 beats per minute, in the maximal heart rate of the highly trained endurance performer.

CHAPTER FOUR

Blood

Blood volume will increase with training but it is unclear to what extent. Studies comparing performers to non-performers have shown improvements of 20–25% irrespective of age and sex, but studies using the same individuals before and after training have shown improvements of only about 8%.

The increase in plasma is greater than the increase in the cells which leads to a relative drop in concentration of the cells. This is advantageous, in that it makes the blood thinner and therefore easier to pump, but it can lead to a wrong diagnosis of anaemia. Since the total amount of red cells, and therefore haemoglobin, has increased with training, more oxygen can be carried in the blood. The plasma has increased to a greater extent and therefore the concentration of red cells has declined. This is the classic definition of anaemia. More strictly, the condition should be referred to as *performer's pseudo-anaemia* and recognised as a normal response to training.

Training is not the only way to alter the oxygen carrying capacity of the blood and thereby improve endurance performance. There are two other means of increasing the amount of haemoglobin:

- Altitude training.
- Blood doping.

Training at altitude stimulates an increase in red cell production to counteract the thinner air and leads to a greater concentration of red cells in the blood. Although more oxygen can be carried when returning to sea level, the blood is thicker and therefore more difficult to pump. Any benefit from carrying more oxygen may be offset by the heart having to do more work to circulate the blood. The increase in red cells alters the biochemistry of the blood and this can be detrimental to performance in some people.

In **blood doping**, a quantity of blood is removed a few weeks before competition and re-infused a few days in advance of the event. In the early days of this technique, only the red cells were re-infused but this has the same disadvantages as altitude training. Diluting the red cells with synthetic plasma can overcome the problem of thickening of the blood and produce a greater blood volume but the biochemical balance is still disrupted.

Muscle

The highly trained endurance performer may be capable of using 50% more oxygen every minute than the untrained, partly because far greater amounts of oxygen can be transported to the muscles and partly because the muscles can use more oxygen. Endurance training has a marked effect on muscle, bringing about considerable improvements in the ability of muscle to extract and use the oxygen passing in the blood capillaries.

Aerobically trained muscle will have up to 50% more capillaries than untrained muscle, thus improving the flow of blood through the muscle and bringing each muscle fibre closer to the supply of oxygen. Oxygen is transported from the blood to the mitochondria by myoglobin (refer back to Section 3.4 on Page 52), a substance very similar to haemoglobin, and some studies have shown this increases in quantity with training. The mitochondria are the *factories* where oxygen is used to release energy from both carbohydrates and fats, and these increase in number and size with training. Since training increases the ability of muscle to utilise oxygen, the blood leaving highly trained muscle will be lower in oxygen.

This specificity of training in muscle explains why cyclists, who produce impressive scores on aerobic fitness tests when measured on the cycle ergometer, may do quite poorly when tested on the treadmill. The same effect is found if runners are tested on cycles. Cyclists and runners might at first sight appear to have much in common and their heart and lungs might be equally well trained. However, they are using different muscles, different fibres within the same muscle, or the same muscle fibres in different ways. Their ability to utilise oxygen is dependent upon how they train.

4.4 Recap

In this chapter, you have studied the ways in which the heart, lungs, blood and muscles respond to aerobic training. This, together with an explanation of the principles of training and an analysis of the aerobic demands of your sport, should have provided you with the necessary knowledge to design an effective aerobic training programme for your sport.

You have had to come to terms with a certain amount of physiological jargon and the following self tester has been designed to help you check whether you have taken all this knowledge on board. Without it, you will not be able to design and monitor aerobic training programmes for your performers.

SELF TESTER 3

1 Identify the four principles of training which are important to aerobic fitness:

   •

   •

   •

   •

2 Explain what is meant by:

   • aerobic threshold:

   • anaerobic threshold:

3 Explain how aerobic training differs for health and for sport:

4 Explain how you would establish the intensity and duration of aerobic training for an elite endurance performer:

5 Explain what is meant by the onset of blood lactate accumulation and why it is significant to aerobic training:

6 The trained performer requires less oxygen
 to do the same task as an untrained performer. True / False

7 Explain the two ways in which training enhances the diffusion rate between alveoli and blood:

   •

   •

8 Complete the table below which describes the maximal values of a 20 year old male:

	Cardiac Output (litres/min)	Stroke Volume (millilitres)	Heart Rate (beats/min)
Untrained			
Trained			

9 Explain what is meant by performer's pseudo-anaemia:

10 Describe three adaptations in muscle with aerobic training:

   •

   •

   •

Self Tester 3

1 Identify the four principles of training which are important to aerobic fitness:
- *Overload.*
- *Progression.*
- *Recovery.*
- *Specificity.*

2 Explain what is meant by:
- *aerobic threshold:*

  Aerobic threshold is the level of exercise where the intensity is sufficient to produce a training effect – about 60% of maximal heart rate for most people.

- *anaerobic threshold:*

  The anaerobic threshold is the point where the aerobic mechanisms become overloaded and anaerobic metabolism begins to play a major part. The anaerobic threshold has been reached in all of us by about 90% of maximum heart rate.

3 Explain how aerobic training differs for health and for sport:

Aerobic training for health trains the slow twitch muscle fibres, whereas for aerobic sports the training should focus on the intermediate and fast twitch fibres.

4 Explain how you would establish the intensity and duration of aerobic training for an elite endurance performer:

Training at, or just below, the anaerobic threshold for 15–35 minutes, or training at 70–90% of maximum heart rate for longer.

5 Explain what is meant by the onset of blood lactate accumulation and why it is significant to aerobic training:

The point where lactic acid accumulates in the blood because it is entering from working muscle faster than it is being removed by other tissues. Aerobic training can be sustained up to this point.

6 The trained performer requires less oxygen to do the same task as an untrained performer.   *True/False*

False (but may be true if the performer has become more skilful).

7 Explain the two ways in which training enhances the diffusion rate between alveoli and blood:
- *A greater surface area for diffusion.*
- *A greater partial pressure difference between alveolus and venous blood.*

8 *Complete the table below which describes the maximal values of a 20 year old male:*

	Cardiac Output (litres/min)	Stroke Volume (millilitres)	Heart Rate (beats/min)
Untrained	25	125	200
Trained	35–40	175–200	195–200

9 *Explain what is meant by performer's pseudo-anaemia:*

The normal response of the performer to endurance training. Blood plasma has increased more than the red cells, lowering the concentration of the red cells even though there are more of them.

10 *Describe three adaptations in muscle with aerobic training:*

- *More capillaries.*
- *More myoglobin.*
- *More and larger mitochondria.*

If you had any difficulty, reread the relevant sections of this chapter, follow up the references, or make a note to ask a tutor, teacher, coach or friend. Other sources of help are given in the next section.

4.5 What Next?

If you would like to study further, the following texts are recommended:

Simple Text

National Coaching Foundation (1997) **Physiology and performance.** 3rd edition. Leeds, National Coaching Foundation. ISBN 0-947850-24-4. *

More Detailed Texts

Fox, EL, Bowers, RW and Foss, ML (1988) **The physiological basis of physical education and athletics.** Dubuque, Iowa, Wm C Brown. ISBN 0-0301-1273-7. *(Out of print)*

Marieb, EN (1999) **Human anatomy and physiology.** New York, Addison Wesley. ISBN 0-20152-263-2. (Unit 4)

Martin, DE and Coe, PN (1997) **Better training for distance runners.** Champaign IL, Human Kinetics. 0-8801-1530-0. (Chapters 2 and 3)

National Coaching Foundation (1998) **A guide to planning coaching programmes.** Leeds, National Coaching Foundation. ISBN 1-902523-00-8.*

---

* Available from Coachwise Ltd (0113 231 1310).

CHAPTER FIVE
Energy

5.0 What's in It for You?

It should be clear by now that oxygen is essential to the contraction of muscle but oxygen itself does not supply energy. Its role is to allow energy to be released from fuel stored in the muscle. Unfortunately, in many sporting situations, the release of energy by oxygen is not fast enough or in large enough quantities to provide all the energy required. The body overcomes this problem to some extent by having two other systems for providing energy, but both of these will only operate for a limited amount of time and the shortfall in oxygen has to be repaid once the intensity of exercise declines. This means that there are three systems of supplying energy for contraction and the importance of each system varies with the different demands of exercise.

This chapter will explain the energy systems and how training can improve their functioning. By the end of this chapter you should be able to:

- explain how energy is made available to sprint type activities in contrast to endurance type activities
- assess how energy is made available in your sport
- suggest ways in which fatigue can be minimised or avoided
- design basic training programmes to improve each of the energy systems.

CHAPTER FIVE

5.1 Adenosine Triphosphate (ATP)

The contraction of muscle is brought about by the interaction of two protein filaments which make up a large proportion of the muscle mass. These two protein filaments, actin and myosin, are drawn into one another by the formation and movement of cross-bridges which temporarily bind the two proteins together and pull one towards the other. This activity, repeated many times down each filament of actin and myosin, and across all of the muscle which might include millions of these protein filaments, results in the shortening of muscle and the creation of force. The following diagram adds further explanation. If this is still unclear, you are strongly advised to study the relevant sections in *An Introduction to the Structure of the Body* or a general physiological text.

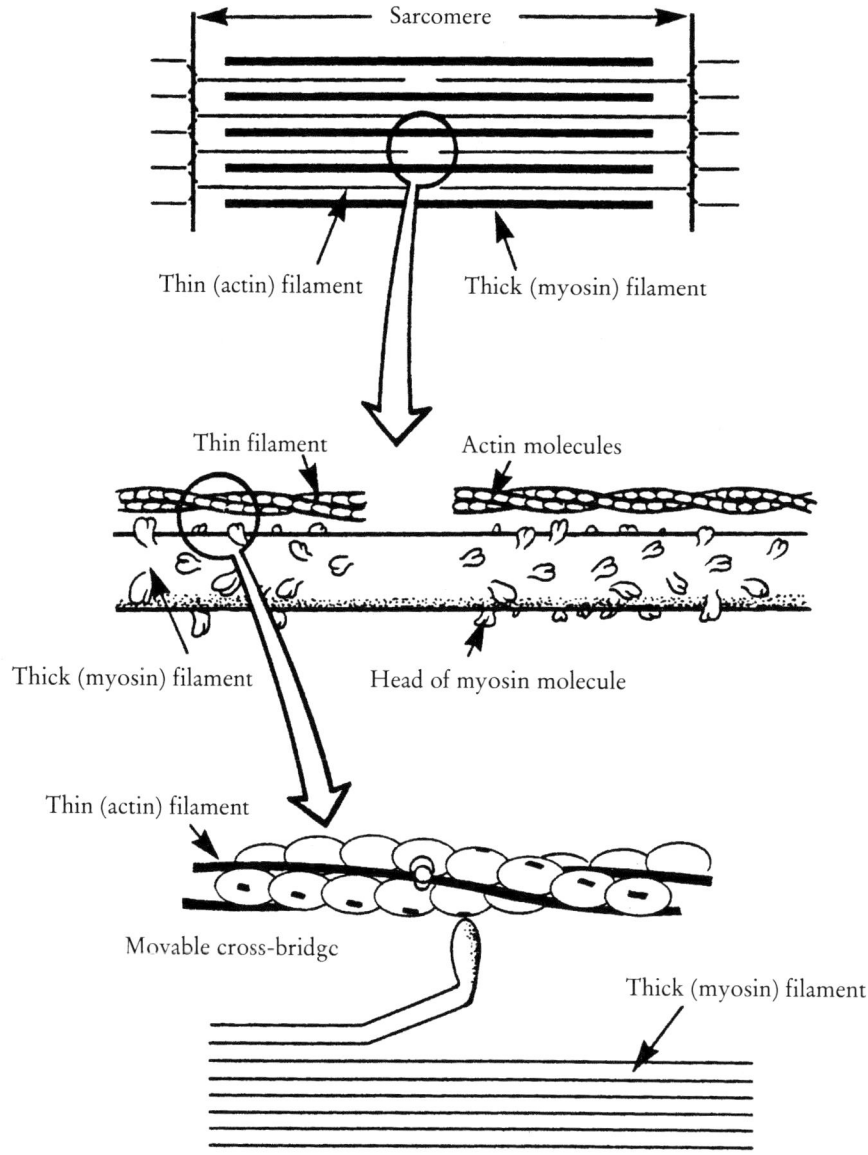

Figure 23: Actin/myosin cross-bridging

The movement of these cross-bridges requires energy. Only one chemical, Adenosine Triphosphate (ATP) found stored in the myosin heads, is able to provide it fast enough and in sufficient quantity to maintain the formation and movement of cross-bridges. Unfortunately, it is only found in relatively small amounts, enough to fuel no more than about one second of intense muscular effort, so it has to be reformed (resynthesized) continually for almost all sporting activities. The energy for the resynthesis of ATP can come from three different sources, the three energy systems.

All muscle activity is fuelled by ATP and the energy for contraction comes from the breakdown of ATP to another chemical, **Adenosine Diphosphate (ADP)**. In this chemical reaction (shown below), one molecule of phosphate (P) splits from one molecule of ATP to leave one molecule of ADP. In the process a relatively large amount of energy is released which is then used by actin and myosin to bring about the contraction.

$$ATP \longrightarrow ADP + P + \text{energy for contraction}$$

This reaction is reversible (ie ATP can be resynthesized from ADP and P) if energy can be provided from elsewhere. This is the function of the energy systems.

ACTIVITY 22

In the weight training room, working at the bench press machine on a set load of about 70% of your maximum, decide what will happen in the following situations:

- Lifting the load repeatedly as fast as you can:

- Lifting the load every two seconds:

- Lifting the load every 20 seconds:

Now turn over.

CHAPTER FIVE

- *Attempting to lift the load as fast as you can repeatedly will lead to exhaustion within only a small number of lifts.*
- *Lifting every two seconds will have increased the total number of lifts considerably but fatigue will have set in after a short period of time.*
- *It is likely that lifting every 20 seconds would result in being able to continue the activity almost indefinitely.*

? Why should these differences occur?

The answer lies in the amount of time available to resynthesize ATP. If there is very little time, there is insufficient oxygen to release energy by aerobic means and the muscle has to use one of the two anaerobic processes. In fact, this is an over-simplification because each of the energy systems does not operate in isolation. Even in the most anaerobic of contractions (eg 100m sprinting), there will be a small contribution from aerobic mechanisms, and in endurance events some of the fibres may be operating anaerobically (eg if there is a change in speed or incline).

5.2 Anaerobic Energy Systems

As the intensity of effort increases above resting levels, there will come a point where not all of the energy required to resynthesize ATP can be provided from fats and carbohydrate broken down in the presence of oxygen. This point, the anaerobic threshold (discussed earlier in Section 4.2 on Page 64), will vary with each individual and is influenced by training. The shortfall in energy has to be met from one of the two anaerobic processes, the **phosphagen energy system** and the **lactate energy system**.

Phosphagen Energy System

The source of energy here is the breakdown of phosphocreatine (creatine phosphate). This does not provide a large amount of energy, perhaps enough for ten seconds of flat-out effort, but it is released quickly so can be used for explosive movements or those bursts of activity which occur in team games. If the intensity of effort is slightly less or is of a stop-start nature (eg in racket game rallies), this energy store may sustain movement for 10–20 seconds. It is very susceptible to training, with up to 300% more phosphocreatine in store after training. Unfortunately, training effects are short-lived so this type of training must be carried out during the competitive season.

You may know that some well-known performers are taking creatine in an attempt to improve performance. There is much controversy over the use of creatine. The following key points (taken from the British Olympic Association's latest Position Statement) should be taken into consideration:

- The Medical Committee are concerned that the BOA should not endorse or encourage the use of creatine supplementation.
- The Medical Committee emphasises the limited situations in which there is a possible enhancement of performance (repetitive sprints). There have been no studies on elite Olympic athletes. The effect on these individuals is not known.
- The dangers of taking large supra-normal doses of creatine that are used in loading regimes is also unquantified. Many *natural* substances when taken in excess are dangerous (eg vitamin A).
- A normal diet provides around 1g/day and probably more in most elite sprinters.
- The BOA Medical Committee does not recommend creatine supplementation.

It is worth noting that the phosphagen stores are half-recovered in thirty seconds and fully recovered in five minutes, provided the person rests. This explains why repeated short sprints are possible, and why a 100m sprinter can run a number of heats of the event on the same day yet maintain quality performances.

There is an implication here for training this energy system. The purpose of training is to overload the system, so the rest interval should be no more than about thirty seconds between repetitive runs if the phosphagen system is to be stimulated. However, if quality work is to be maintained in training, there should be recovery periods of at least five minutes from time to time to refuel the phosphagen stores fully.

Lactate Energy System

This system is so named because the end product of the breakdown of the fuel used (glycogen) is lactic acid. An alternative name is anaerobic glycolysis because glycogen is broken down (glycolysis), when there is a shortage of oxygen. An increase in acidity in the muscle cell, caused by the production of lactic acid, will interfere with the chemical reactions to such an extent that the cell stops working until the excess acidity can be removed. This can easily be demonstrated.

CHAPTER FIVE

ACTIVITY 23

Try the following activities which show how lactic acid builds up in muscle in two very different types of contractions.

1. Fill a shopping bag or other suitable container with a heavy weight. Hold the bag at arm's length for as long as possible (the weight in the bag should allow you to hold it for at least thirty seconds but no longer than two minutes).

   Describe how you feel at the point when you fatigue:

   After fifteen seconds rest, find out if you can repeat the activity, and if so, note how long:

2. Perform sit-ups to a regular rhythm (about one sit-up every two seconds) until you fatigue (between thirty seconds and two minutes).

   Describe how you feel at the point when you fatigue:

   After fifteen seconds rest, find out if you can repeat the activity, and if so, note how long:

   Now turn over.

In each of these activities, your muscles have produced large amounts of lactic acid. Eventually this has stopped the chemical reactions necessary to resynthesize ATP.

- *In the bag carrying task, the muscles which were working to hold the weight remained contracted throughout, preventing blood entering the muscle and bringing in oxygen. Therefore, the muscle had to work anaerobically (an anaerobic isometric contraction[1]), and in a short period of time it fatigued. It is probable that at the end of the task you flexed and extended your arm a few times, so encouraging the passage of blood into and out of the muscle. After 15 seconds some of the lactic acid had been washed out of the muscle, the concentration had dropped sufficiently to allow further contraction to take place, and you were able to continue the task for a little longer.*

- *A similar situation occurred when you carried out the sit-ups, except here of course the muscles were working isotonically and there was opportunity for blood to enter and leave the muscle. Unfortunately, the removal of lactic acid in the blood was not fast enough and it was being added by the contractions to carry out the task, so the net effect was a build up of lactic acid and the inevitable fatigue occurred. After 15 seconds of rest, quite a lot of lactic acid would have been washed out of the muscle but there would still be more in the muscle than when you began the sit-ups. Consequently you would have been able to do some more, but not as many as the first time.*

It is interesting to note that training of the appropriate type can improve performance and does so by:

- increasing the lactic acid tolerance of the muscle (greater concentrations can be endured before contractions cease)
- improving the ability to remove lactic acid from the working muscles.

Lactic acid is produced because the muscle is working at a level where the force produced by the aerobic slow twitch fibres (ST) is not enough. The point at which the anaerobic fast twitch fibres (FT) have to be recruited varies between individuals, because it depends upon the relative percentages of ST and FT fibres in the muscle (a genetic factor):

- Performers with a high percentage of ST fibres will be able to work at a greater intensity before building up large quantities of lactic acid but their maximum work intensity will be quite low because they have fewer FT fibres to call upon thereafter.

- Performers with a high percentage of FT fibres will start to build up lactate at lower work intensities but have the potential for a higher maximum work intensity because many more FT fibres can be called upon. However, this type of performer will fatigue sooner. Consequently, the good endurance performer who has plenty of ST fibres can sustain a higher steady pace than the sprinter but the sprinter can produce a faster maximum speed. This is shown in the graph on the opposite page.

1 For more information about types of contraction see the NCF Home Study Pack *An Introduction to the Structure of the Body.*

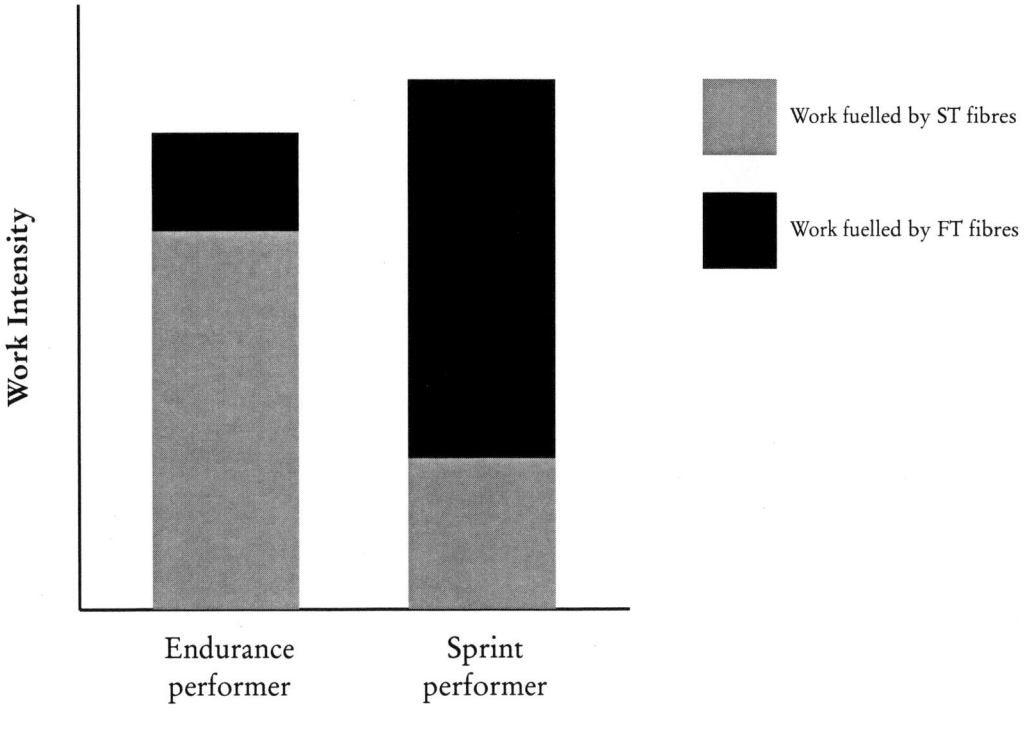

Figure 24: Relative contributions of work fuelled by ST and FT fibres to total work intensity

FT fibres are using the same fuel (glycogen) as ST fibres but their specialist ability to contract rapidly carries with it a handicap. Glycogen is broken down as far as pyruvic acid to release energy for contraction but the aerobic pathway is not open because FT fibres lack ability to use oxygen. Instead, pyruvic acid is converted into lactic acid and this accumulates until the muscle cell can no longer contract. This may take 30–40 seconds in the untrained but it is very responsive to training.

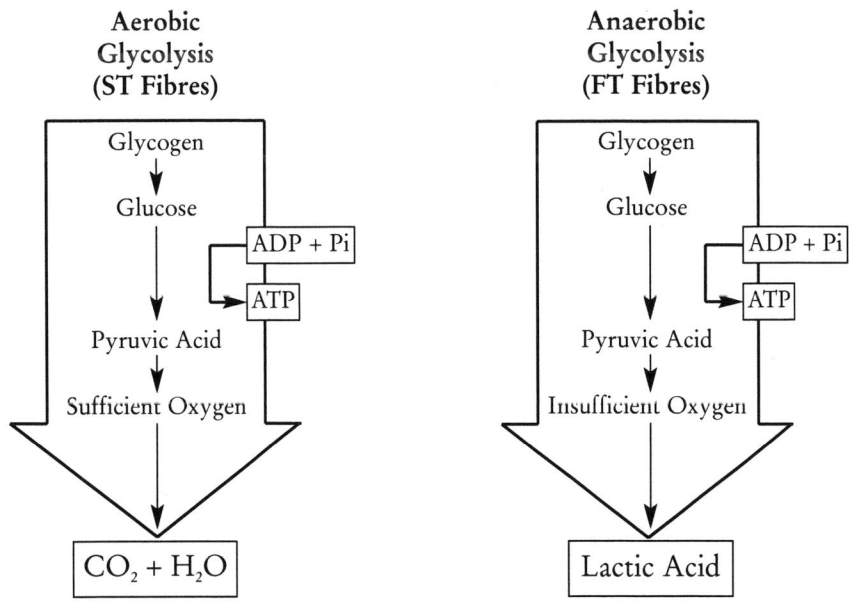

Figure 25: Breakdown of glycogen in the presence and absence of oxygen

CHAPTER FIVE

The anaerobic performer's problem is balancing lactic acid production and removal. In fact, the performer can do very little about the production of lactic acid because this appears to be much the same in the trained and untrained for the same level of work. Fortunately, training will improve the ability to tolerate larger amounts of lactic acid so more work can be done. It is not known to what extent this is a physiological improvement in the muscle or a psychological adaptation to live with more pain.

The most significant improvement is in the ability to remove lactic acid as it accumulates. Although some lactic acid can be recycled within its own cell because there is some aerobic capacity in all FT fibres, the majority passes out of the cell. Some of this is processed in neighbouring ST fibres but most moves into the bloodstream. Here, further lactic acid can be removed by chemicals in the blood, producing carbon dioxide which is breathed out, and much of the rest is transported either to other muscle tissue or organs such as the liver and heart.

It should be clear that it is important to maintain good blood flow through working muscles after the major effort has ceased. This emphasises the importance of cooling down. However, there is another implication which is crucial to those sports where there is repeated anaerobic work. Boxing, for example, involves three minutes vigorous activity, much of it anaerobic, followed by a one minute recovery time between rounds. This time should be used to wash out as much lactic acid as possible. If the boxer sits down, the working muscles will reduce the blood flow very rapidly and lactic acid will not be removed very efficiently. It has been shown that continuous low-level exercise is much better so the boxer would be wiser to remain standing between rounds, keeping the limbs moving in low-level work. Is there a similar situation in your sport? What should squash players do between games?

ACTIVITY 24

The following table gives examples of anaerobic activities, assesses the duration of the anaerobic phase, the type of follow-on activity the performers tend to do and the type of follow-on activity they would be advised to do.

Study these and then add your own sport (and/or a range of different sports):

Sport/Activity	Duration of Anaerobic Phase	Typical Follow-on Activity	Better Follow-on Activity
Boxing	Three min vigorous activity	One min rest when they tend to sit down	Remain standing and move limbs
Squash	Repeated 10–20 second rallies	Sit on floor for one minute between games	Remain standing and move limbs
Volleyball	Repeated 15–30 second rallies	Substituted – sit down	Keep moving for few minutes
Rugby forward	30 second ruck/maul	Stand when whistle blows	Avoid standing still
Your sport:			

Now turn over.

You may be surprised how many times a period of anaerobic work is followed by inactivity. This may sometimes be constrained by the rules of the game but more often it is probably tradition. You should have been able to suggest alternative follow-on activities that would speed up recovery.

5.3 Aerobic Energy Systems

In any activity which is sustained for a period of time (eg running, cycling or swimming), there must be sufficient oxygen present to provide all of the energy requirements, otherwise the performer would slow down. This is true of all endurance sports. The skill of the endurance performer is to be able to judge precisely the point where additional energy from anaerobic processes is required and to work just below this threshold. By so doing, the performer is able to work at the highest possible speed without developing fatigue from a build-up of lactic acid in the muscle.

The onset of **anaerobic glycolysis** (the breakdown of glycogen to release energy when not enough oxygen is present) varies between individuals and is probably specific to the type of activity (eg it may differ between running and cycling). It is highly trainable and therefore the endurance performer should devote a considerable amount of training time to pushing back this anaerobic threshold.

Aerobic energy is not only important to endurance performers, for many other activities have a large aerobic element. In field games, for example, which are best described as multi-sprint sports, considerable demand is placed upon aerobic energy because many of the movements are sustained at a high level. Even in activities which are essentially anaerobic (eg 400 metre running), aerobic training is crucial because a well-developed aerobic system helps to delay the onset of lactic acid accumulation in the muscle and to improve the *wash-out*.

There is a further benefit which applies also to the *phosphagen performer* (the power performer such as the thrower, jumper or sprinter). The high intensity training of this anaerobic performer will only be of value if it stresses the working muscles. A poorly developed cardiovascular system will lead to fatigue here before the muscles are adequately stressed, seriously limiting the value of the anaerobic training.

ACTIVITY 25

Attempts have been made to find out the relative importance of aerobic energy to a wide range of sports. Using the table below, select a variety of sports/activities (team, individual, water-based, non-competitive, including your own) and estimate the relative aerobic and anaerobic contributions:

Sport/Activity	% Aerobic	% Anaerobic
Tennis		
Your sport:		

Now turn over.

Compare your ideas with the table below.

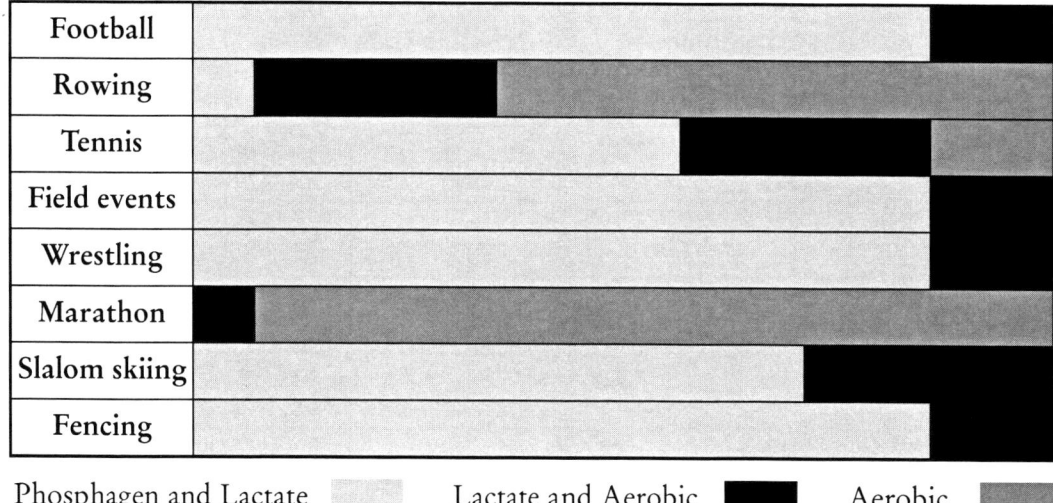

Table 3: An approximation of the aerobic/anaerobic breakdown of sports and athletics

Phosphagen and Lactate   Lactate and Aerobic   Aerobic

A table like this should be viewed cautiously. In team games, for example, so much depends upon the nature of each specific game (eg the quality of the opposition, weather conditions, scoring). Such attempts to produce accurate information should only be used to provide guidelines for designing training programmes.

The aerobic energy system is completely dependent upon the supply of oxygen by the oxygen transport system. Oxygen arriving at the muscle is picked up by myoglobin and transported to the mitochondria where aerobic glycolysis takes place. In anaerobic glycolysis, glycogen is broken down to pyruvic acid, and this still occurs when oxygen is present. However, the presence of oxygen ensures that pyruvic acid does not degrade into lactic acid. Instead, pyruvic acid is converted to a substance called acetyl co-enzyme A and from here enters a complex series of chemical reactions called the **Krebs cycle.** When you burn fat, as you do in low intensity work, the fat is broken down to acetyl co-enzyme A and then follows the same pathway.

The Krebs cycle releases its energy relatively slowly, hence aerobic glycolysis cannot support very high intensity work, but it does so in abundance. Whereas anaerobic glycolysis will only release enough energy from one molecule of glycogen to resynthesize 3ATP, aerobic glycolysis provides energy to resynthesize 38ATP from one molecule of glycogen. Since the stores of glycogen are limited, perhaps supporting aerobic glycolysis for about 60–90 minutes in the poorly trained performer, it makes sense to ensure that as much of it as possible is used aerobically. The individual who runs a race at varying pace, often dipping into anaerobic glycolysis, will fatigue more quickly than the steady-pace runner.

Fortunately, training has beneficial effects. Glycogen stores can be increased as much as threefold, and the well-trained endurance performer is able to spare the use of glycogen by burning a greater percentage of fat. Figure 26 shows this effect.

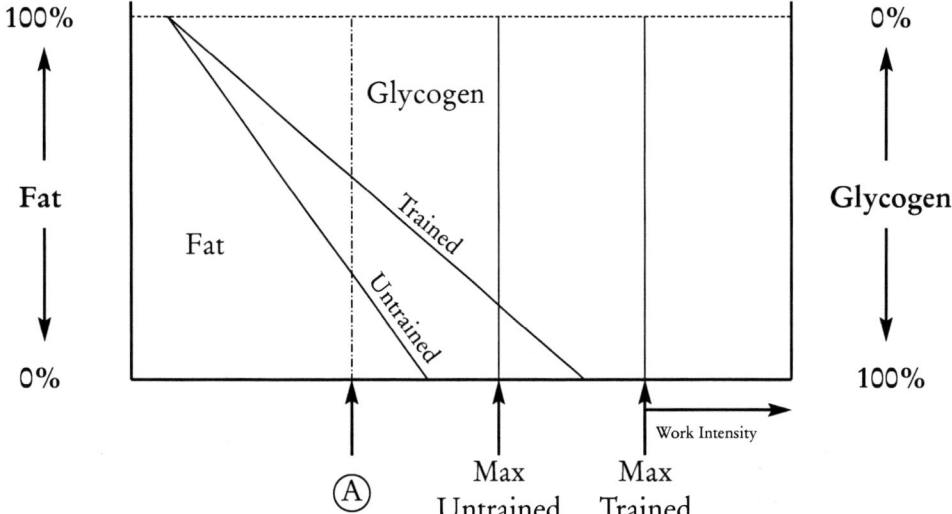

At any sub-maximal work intensity (eg Ⓐ) the trained performer spares more glycogen by burning more fat.

Figure 26: Percentage contribution from fat/CHO before and after training

5.4 Contribution of each Energy System

Although it is convenient to explain each of the energy systems as if they operate in isolation, this is not the case. It is almost certainly true that in every muscle contraction, there is a contribution from each of the three systems. It may help to look at the contribution of the three energy systems in relation to the duration of the event, which is shown below.

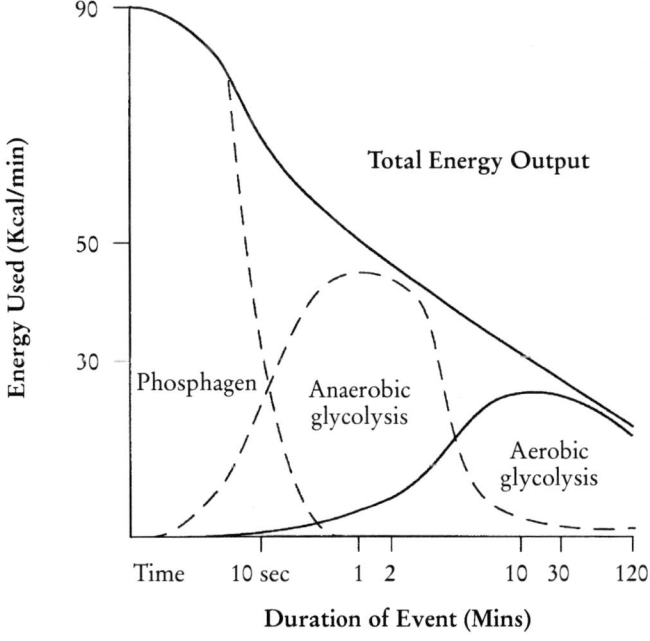

Figure 27: Graph of energy released with respect to time

CHAPTER FIVE

If the event lasts for only a few seconds (eg in sprinting), almost all the energy to resynthesize ATP comes from the phosphagen system. An event lasting a minute (eg 400 metre hurdles) would use considerable amounts of energy from anaerobic glycolysis. There is also a significant contribution from aerobic glycolysis because there is some oxygen available, and some phosphagen energy may be used if there is a maximal effort at some point during the event such as a sprint finish. Events lasting more than about three minutes (eg 1500 metres) depending upon fitness and individual differences, are largely fuelled from aerobic glycolysis.

ACTIVITY 26

To check your understanding of the energy systems, complete the following table to show the relative contributions of the three energy systems, using the code:

***   a lot

**   significant amount

*   hardly any

	Energy System		
	Phosphagen	Lactate	Aerobic
Shot put			
25 mile cycle race (hilly course)			
Channel swim			
Competitive badminton			
Your sport			

Now turn over.

Check your answers with the following table:

	Energy System		
	Phosphagen	*Lactate*	Aerobic
Shot put	* * *	*	*
25 mile cycle race (hilly course)	* *	* *	* * *
Channel swim	*	*	* * *
Competitive badminton	* * *	* *	* * *
Your sport			

The shot put is an explosive event using phosphagen energy almost exclusively. The cycle race is mainly aerobic but there would be a significant contribution from the lactate system on long hill climbs, and from the phosphagen system on short, fast climbs and the sprint finish. The channel swim is exclusively an aerobic event. Obviously, the nature of the badminton match will effect the source of energy. At the highest level of competition, both aerobic and phosphagen energy play an important part, with some contribution from the lactate system if there are long rallies.

You may wish to check the relative contribution of each energy system in your sport with a senior coach, your tutor or teacher.

5.5 Application to your Sport

The information you have gained in this chapter is of limited use unless you are able to apply it to your own sport. To do this, you first need to analyse your sport to assess which system to train and the amount of time to devote to this training. Then you can use the principles of training to design a programme. The next two activities will help you to get started.

ACTIVITY 27

Complete the following training session to improve the speed of a 100 metre sprinter:

Performer: 100 metre sprinter

Energy system: _____

Warm-up:
Five minutes gentle jog
Five minutes joint mobilisation
Five minutes stretching
Five x fifty metre acceleration sprints (jog to 90% max)

Set 1: Ten maximal sprints:

Duration: _____

Recovery time between runs: _____

Activity between runs: _____

Time between sets: _____

Set 2: Eight maximal sprints:

Duration: _____

Recovery time between runs: _____

Activity between runs: _____

Time between sets: _____

Cool-down:
Three minutes jog
Three minutes stretching

Now turn over.

Compare your answers and read the explanation:

Energy system: phosphagen energy system.

For both sets: Duration: 10–12 seconds.
Recovery time between runs: 30 seconds.
Activity between runs: standing, walking.
Time between sets: 5 minutes.

- *The duration of each run should be close to the event time (ie 10–12 seconds), although there may be some training sessions devoted to shorter runs to develop speed at the start of a race.*
- *The recovery time between runs should only allow partial recovery of the energy store. Since phosphagen energy is half recovered in 30 seconds, this would allow some recovery and yet still stress the system.*
- *Recovery time should be spent in low level activity (eg standing, walking), so that further phosphagen energy is not being used.*
- *A five minute rest between sets is recommended to allow full recovery of energy so that quality work can be done in the second set.*

This activity is an example of what you might do to overload a performer in one training session to produce quality work of benefit to performance. The next step would be to look at the frequency of these training sessions and then to consider the other principles of training described in Chapter Four. Now comes the difficult part which is applying all this to your own sport. The next activity will guide you through this process.

ACTIVITY 28

1 Analyse your sport to assess which energy system to train (eg consider the intensity, duration and frequency of the bursts of activity):

2 Specify the amount of time needed for this training:

3 Use the principles of training to design a programme to train this energy system for a period of three weeks. State whether the training is off-season, pre-season or in-season and provide some detail of each session:

Sport: Off-season / Pre-season / In-season

Session _____ Week: Day:	
Session _____ Week: Day:	
Session _____ Week: Day:	
Session _____ Week: Day:	
Session _____ Week: Day:	
Session _____ Week: Day:	
Session _____ Week: Day:	
Session _____ Week: Day:	
Session _____ Week: Day:	
Session _____ Week: Day:	

Continued...

CHAPTER FIVE

Session _____ Week: Day:	
Session _____ Week: Day:	
Session _____ Week: Day:	
Session _____ Week: Day:	
Session _____ Week: Day:	
Session _____ Week: Day:	
Session _____ Week: Day:	
Session _____ Week: Day:	
Session _____ Week: Day:	
Session _____ Week: Day:	
Session _____ Week: Day:	

You will need to check the training programme you have devised with your tutor or a senior coach in your sport.

5.6 Recap

In this chapter, you have had a chance to consider the energy demands of your sport and the relative contribution of each energy system. You should be familiar with the benefits and drawbacks of each system and tried designing training programmes to help your performers develop the appropriate energy system. You should now be in a position to look at training for your sport more critically and, as your confidence and knowledge grow with further reading and study, be able to design successful training programmes.

To test how well you have grasped the principles of the three energy systems and the implications for training, try the following self tester.

SELF TESTER 4

1 Explain why ATP is the immediate store of energy in muscle:

2 The energy systems make ATP.   True / False

3 Suggest which energy system is being most strongly taxed when doing sit-ups continuously for one minute:

4 Anaerobic glycolysis is the breakdown of the carbohydrate
  store in muscle in the absence of oxygen.   True / False

5 Complete the diagram below by placing each of the energy systems in the appropriate place.

Speed of release:
Fast ←————————————————→ Slow

Amount of energy available:
Small ←————————————————→ Large

6 The diagram below shows the contribution of the energy stores at a particular moment in time.

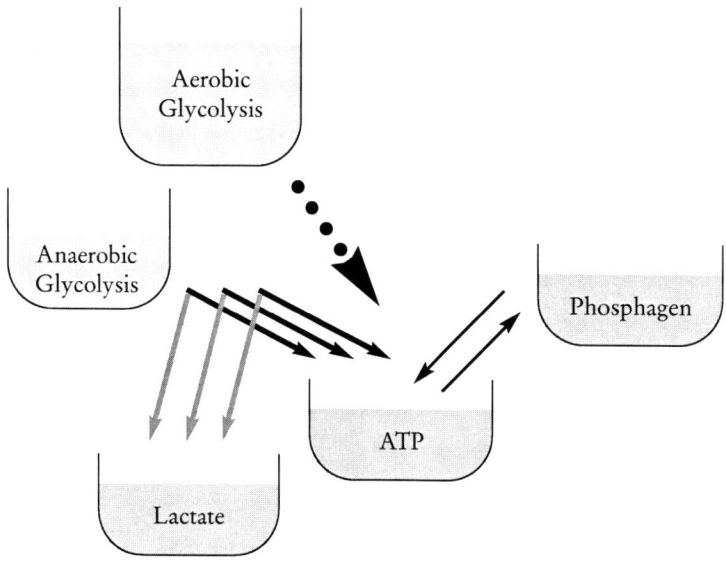

Figure 28: Fuel pots for lactate energy

Suggest three different activities which are fuelled in this way:

-

-

-

Explain how fatigue would occur:

7 After a period of training, the performer produces
   less lactic acid at the same level of work. True / False

8 If the carbohydrate store in muscle (glycogen), becomes exhausted, the endurance
   performer has to slow down. Describe two ways in which training can help to
   prevent this from happening:

   •

   •

Self Tester 4

1. *Explain why ATP is the immediate store of energy in muscle:*

   Because it is located on the myosin heads and is the only fuel for contraction.

2. *The energy systems make ATP.*   True / False

   False – They provide energy and this energy is used to remake ATP from ADP and P.

3. *Suggest which energy system is being most strongly taxed when doing sit-ups continuously for one minute:*

   Lactic acid.

4. *Anaerobic glycolysis is the breakdown of the carbohydrate store in muscle in the absence of oxygen.*   True / False

   True.

5. *Complete the diagram below by placing each of the energy systems in the appropriate place.*

   Speed of release:
   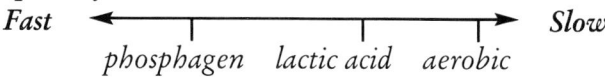

   Amount of energy available:
   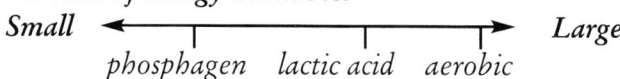

6. *The diagram below shows the contribution of the energy stores at a particular moment in time.*

   Suggest three different activities which are fuelled in this way:

   Any activities which are sustained at a high level for 30–60 seconds (eg 400 metre running, wrestling, 100 metre swim).

   Explain how fatigue would occur:

   Lactic acid would build up in the muscle preventing further contraction.

7. *After a period of training the performer produces less lactic acid at the same level of work.*   True / False

   False. The same amount is produced but there is faster removal and greater concentrations can be tolerated.

8 If the carbohydrate store in muscle (glycogen) becomes exhausted, the endurance performer has to slow down. Describe two ways in which training can help to prevent this from happening:

- *The store of glycogen is increased with training.*
- *The trained performer spares the use of glycogen by burning more fat.*

If you had any difficulty, reread the relevant sections of this chapter, follow up some of the references, or make a note to ask a tutor, teacher, coach or friend. Other sources of help are given in the next section.

5.7 What Next?

If you have successfully worked your way through this pack, you should have a better understanding of your sport and be more able to prepare relevant fitness training programmes. You will have a good general knowledge of how the lungs, heart and blood-vessels work to deliver oxygen to working muscle, and appreciate how energy is released in muscle under different exercise conditions.

There is still much to learn of course, and it is important to remember that knowledge in this area is growing rapidly and some of the things currently believed to be true may be disproved with future research. Although many aspects of training are effective, the reasons are not always known. Therefore, it is important not only to extend your knowledge but also regularly to update it.

If you would like to study further, the following references are recommended:

BOA Position Statement on Creatine Supplementation (www.hpcoaching.net or www.ncf.org.uk-high performance)

Fox, EL, Bowers, RW and Foss, ML (1988) **The physiological basis of physical education and athletics.** Dubuque, Iowa, Wm C Brown. ISBN 0-0301-1273-7. *(Out of print)*

Katch, FI and McArdle, WD (1993) **Nutrition, weight control and exercise.** Philadelphia, Lea & Febiger. ISBN 0-8121-1555-4.

Lamb, DR (1984) **Physiology of exercise.** London, Collier Macmillan. ISBN 0-02-367210-2. *(Out of print)*

Other home study packs designed to help you understand sport and sports performance include:

Farrally, M (1995) **An introduction to the structure of the body.** Leeds, National Coaching Foundation. ISBN 1-85060-1690. *

Galvin, B and Ledger, P (1998) **A guide to planning coaching programmes.** Leeds, National Coaching Foundation, ISBN 1-902523-00-8. *

Sprunt, K (2000) **An introduction to sports mechanics.** 3rd edition. Leeds, National Coaching Foundation. ISBN 1-902523-34-2. *

Details of all NCF resources are available from:

Coachwise Ltd
Units 2/3, Chelsea Close
Off Amberley Road
Armley
Leeds LS12 4HW
Tel: 0113 231 1310
Fax: 0113 231 231 9606

For direct bookings on NCF workshops at Premier Coaching Centres, please contact:

Wokshop Booking Centre
Units 2/3, Chelsea Close
Off Amberley Road
Armley, Leeds LS12 4HW
Tel: 0845 601 3054
Fax: 0113 231 9606

The NCF also produces a technical journal, *Faster Higher, Stronger (FHS)* and an information update service for coaches (*in*FORM). Details of these services are available from:

The National Coaching Foundation
114 Cardigan Road
Headingley
Leeds LS6 3BJ
Tel: 0113 274 4802
Fax: 0113 275 5019
E-mail: coaching@ncf.org.uk
Internet; www.ncf.org.uk

* Available from Coachwise Ltd (0113 231 1310).

NCF coach workshops and resources (complimentary with the corresponding workshop) include:

NCF Coach Workshop	Resource
Analysing your Coaching	Analysing your Coaching (home study)
Coaching Children and Young People	Coaching Young Performers
Coaching Disabled Performers	Coaching Disabled Performers (home study)
Coaching Methods and Communication	The Successful Coach
Fitness and Training	Physiology and Performance
Fuelling Performers	Fuelling Performers
Goal-setting and Planning	Planning Coaching Programmes (home study)
Good Practice and Child Protection	Protecting Children (home study)
Improving Practices and Skill	Improving Practices and Skill
Injury Prevention and Management	Sports Injury
Motivaton and Mental Toughness	Motivation and Mental Toughness
Observation, Analysis and Video	Observation, Analysis and Video

NCF performance coach workshops and resources (complimentary with the corresponding workshop) include:

NCF Performance Coach Workshop	Resource
Field-based Fitness Testing	A Guide to Field Based Fitness Testing
Performance Profiling	Performance Profiling (audiotape and booklet)
Imagery Training	Imagery Training

CHAPTER FIVE

For details of all NCF workshops, contact your nearest Regional Training Unit or home countries office:

East
    Tel: 01234 261547
    Fax: 01234 214457

West Midlands
    Tel: 0121 414 3379/414 7613
    Fax: 0121 414 7645

London
    Tel: 020 7594 9069
    Fax: 020 7594 9070

North
    Tel: 0191 374 7820
    Fax: 0191 374 7434

North West
    Tel: 01695 584657
    Fax: 01695 584710

South
    Tel: 01628 475510
    Fax: 01628 475512

Yorkshire
    Tel: 0113 283 1763
    Fax: 0113 283 3170

East Midlands
    Tel: 01509 223493
    Fax: 01509 223950

South East
    Tel: 01323 411186
    Fax: 01323 644653

South West
    Tel: 01225 444823
    Fax: 01225 561547

Wales
    Tel: 02920 300500
    Fax: 02920 300600

Northern Ireland
    Tel: 028 9038 1222
    Fax: 028 9068 2757

Scotland
    Tel: 0131 317 1091/317 7200
    Fax: 0131 317 7202

APPENDIX A
Multiple Choice Questions

If you wish to check your own understanding and knowledge, complete the following questions.

Shade in the box alongside your chosen answer(s). For each statement there may be more than one correct response.

1   **Physiology includes the study of:**
    - [ ] a   muscle structure
    - [ ] b   the body's fuel supplies
    - [ ] c   how the body functions
    - [ ] d   sporting actions.

2   **The oxygen transport system is essential because:**
    - [ ] a   the body's muscles need oxygen to function efficiently
    - [ ] b   it controls the amount of fuel delivered to the muscles
    - [ ] c   oxygen cannot reach the muscle cells by diffusion
    - [ ] d   it transmits nerve impulses to the working muscles.

3   **The oxygen concentration of the blood is greatest in the:**
    - [ ] a   aorta
    - [ ] b   veins
    - [ ] c   pulmonary artery
    - [ ] d   right ventricle.

4   **The left side of the heart:**
    - [ ] a   pumps blood to the lungs
    - [ ] b   receives oxygen depleted blood from the muscles
    - [ ] c   is the strongest side of the heart
    - [ ] d   forms part of the systemic circulation.

5   **The substance in red blood cells with a high affinity for oxygen is:**
    - [ ] a   plasma
    - [ ] b   carbon dioxide
    - [ ] c   haemoglobin
    - [ ] d   glucose.

APPENDIX A

6   Why is the cool-down important?
 ❑ a It prevents blood pooling in the limbs.
 ❑ b It reduces the likelihood of dizziness or fainting.
 ❑ c It assists blood pooling in the limbs.
 ❑ d It allows waste products to accumulate in the muscles.

7   What effect does exercise intensity have on the tidal flow of air in and out of the lungs?
 ❑ a It decreases.
 ❑ b It remains constant.
 ❑ c It increases.
 ❑ d It increases, but only during anaerobic exercise.

8   Cardiac output is:
 ❑ a the amount of deoxygenated blood pumped by the heart
 ❑ b the stroke volume minus the systolic output
 ❑ c the product of the stroke volume and systolic output
 ❑ d the best measure of the blood supply and demand.

9   An increase in tidal volume is brought about by:
 ❑ a a greater depth of breathing
 ❑ b a decrease in residual volume
 ❑ c an increase in residual volume
 ❑ d an increased rate of breathing.

10   Altitude training increases:
 ❑ a the size of the heart
 ❑ b the concentration of haemoglobin in the blood
 ❑ c the ability of the cardiovascular system to meet exercise demands
 ❑ d the capacity of the lungs.

11   Coaches and their performers should be able to monitor heart rate because it is the best indicator of:
 ❑ a cardiac output
 ❑ b cardiac output and recovery
 ❑ c lung capacity
 ❑ d training intensity and recovery.

APPENDIX A

12 A performer's maximal heart rate can be estimated by the following calculation:
- ❏ a 220 minus age.
- ❏ b 220 plus age.
- ❏ c 220 divided by age.
- ❏ d 140 plus resting heart rate.

13 Anaerobic means:
- ❏ a with oxygen
- ❏ b without carbon dioxide
- ❏ c with oxygen and carbon dioxide
- ❏ d with a shortage of oxygen.

14 The upper limit above which the body can no longer sustain aerobic exercise is known as the:
- ❏ a aerobic threshold
- ❏ b aerobic capacity
- ❏ c anaerobic threshold
- ❏ d maximum heart rate.

15 All muscle activity is fuelled by the chemical:
- ❏ a Adenosine Diphoshate
- ❏ b Phosphagen
- ❏ c Myosin
- ❏ d Adenosine Triphosphate.

16 The breakdown of phosphocreatine (creatine phosphate) yields enough energy to sustain high intensity activity for:
- ❏ a up to ten seconds
- ❏ b 10–20 seconds
- ❏ c two minutes
- ❏ d as long as glycogen is available.

17 The energy systems available to the performer are the:
- ❏ a phosphagen, lactate and aerobic glycolysis systems
- ❏ b phosphagen, lactate and anaerobic glycolysis systems
- ❏ c lactate, anaerobic and aerobic energy systems
- ❏ d aerobic and phosphagen systems.

APPENDIX A

18 The relative value of each energy system is determined by:
- ❑ a the duration of the activity
- ❑ b the level of glycogen stores
- ❑ c the intensity of the activity
- ❑ d the sex of the performer.

19 Which of the following sports are fuelled predominately by the aerobic energy system?
- ❑ a Shot put, long-distance swim, high jump.
- ❑ b High jump, gymnastics, weightlifting.
- ❑ c Sprint cycle race, slalom skiing, competitive badminton.
- ❑ d 25 mile cycle race, marathon run, rowing.

20 Well trained performers are able to:
- ❑ a increase their maximum heart rate
- ❑ b utilise a greater percentage of fat
- ❑ c reduce their glycogen stores
- ❑ d delay the onset of glycogen depletion.

The answers can be found on Page 126.

APPENDIX B
Case Study

Select one performer you currently coach. For this performer, identify the energy needs of his/her event or position (team sports) and the relative contribution of each energy system to performance. Describe how a training programme (eg over two or three months) would prepare this performer physiologically for competition. Explain how this programme would fit within the overall training and competition season. When appropriate, adopt this programme, monitor its effectiveness and evaluate its impact on the performer.

Answers to multiple choice questions:

1: a, b & c	5: c	9: a & d	13: d	17: a
2: a & c	6: a & b	10: b & c	14: c	18: a & c
3: a	7: c	11: d	15: d	19: d
4: c & d	8: c & d	12: a	16: a	20: b & d

APPENDIX C
National Occupational Standards for Coaching, Teaching and Instructing

The National Occupational Standards for Coaching, Teaching and Instructing (NOS) are based around a number of competencies associated with planning, delivering and evaluating coaching sessions and programmes. The standards are used as part of national governing bodies' coach education awards and as the definition of competence for Scottish/National Vocational Qualifications (S/NVQs) in coaching, teaching and instructing. S/NVQs at Levels 2 and 3 are available in a number of sports. The NCF has developed its Coach Development Programme around these standards. NCF workshops and resources aim to provide the underpinning knowledge for coaches who wish to meet the competencies of the standards. They also give coaches guidelines on how to apply this knowledge to their coaching practice.

This resource, *An Introduction to Sports Physiology*, has been designed to support the following units of the Level 3 NOS:

Unit B12 Promote the adoption and maintenance of regular physical activity
B12.2 Promote the benefits of regular exercise and opportunities to take part
B12.3 Build confidence for participation in regular physical activity

Unit D49 Plan, manage and evaluate a basic physical conditioning programme
D49.1 Collect and analyse information to plan basic physical conditioning programmes
D49.2 Manage and evaluate field tests of physical condition
D49.3 Develop basic physical conditioning programmes to meet goals
D49.4 Manage and evaluate basic physical conditioning programmes to meet identified goals

For further information on the National Occupational Standards for Coaching, Teaching and Instructing at Level 3, contact the National Coaching Foundation or SPRITO at the following addresses:

The National Coaching Foundation
114 Cardigan Road
Headingley
Leeds
LS6 3BJ
Tel: 0113 274 4802
Fax: 0113 275 5019

E-mail: coaching@ncf.org.uk
Internet: www.ncf.org.uk

The National Training Organisation for
   Sport, Recreation and Allied Occupations
24 Stephenson Way
London
NW1 2HD
Tel: 0207 388 7755
Fax: 0207 388 9733

E-mail: the.nto@sprito.org.uk

Notes:

Notes: